Coping with

MEDIA
VIOLENCE

Holly Cefrey

The Rosen Publishing Group, Inc.
New York

Published in 2001 by The Rosen Publishing Group, Inc.
29 East 21st Street, New York, NY 10010

Cover photo © Cindy Reiman

Library of Congress Cataloging-in-Publication Data

Cefrey, Holly.
Coping with media violence / by Holly Cefrey.— 1st ed.
p. cm. — (Coping)
Includes bibliographical references and index.
ISBN 0-8239-2893-4 (library binding)
1. Violence in mass media. 2. Mass media—Social aspects—United States. [1. Violence in mass media. 2. Mass media—Social aspects.] I.Title. II. Series.
P96.V52 U64 2001
303.6'0973—dc21
　　　　　　　　　　　　　　　　　　　　2001001657

Manufactured in the United States of America

Contents

Introduction   1

1   Mass Media and Our Society   5

2   What Is Violence in the Media?   21

3   Getting Exposed to Media Violence   35

4   Effects of Media Violence   51

5   Understanding Your Role in Media Violence   63

6   Seeing Through Violence in Positive Ways   80

Glossary   95

For More Information   96

For Further Reading   102

Index   104

Introduction

Trish's radio alarm clock wakes her every school day morning. It's set to the city's most popular music station. On any morning she will wake to songs known for their violent themes from artists such as Eminem and Marilyn Manson. Eminem's lyrics " . . . [beep] I'm-a kill you . . ." are repeated in a rhythmic pattern as she wakes from a night's sleep. "It's played on a radio station that is run by adults so it must not be that bad," she reasons to herself.

On the school bus, Trish talks with her friends about movies. Her friend Taylor just saw the trailer for the newest horror film. "It's so cool, he kills a guy with a bar glass . . . I can't wait to see it," Taylor squeals. Taylor's older brother sneaks Taylor and his friends in to see the graphic R-rated movies. "Taylor's brother is really cool, so it must be all right to see fight films," she ponders.

While walking to her locker, Trish glances inside of other students' open lockers. Pictures of women in submissive or captive poses line some of the guys' lockers. Other lockers have pictures with rap stars encircled by kneeling women wearing very little

1

clothing. The women seem to be worshipping the rap stars in their defensive, muscle-flexing poses. "Nobody tells them to take the pictures down, so I guess it's not that big a deal," she thinks to herself.

While in class, Phillip, one of the most popular guys in school, takes off his coat. A loud clang is heard as a knife falls from his coat to the floor. Phillip quickly picks up the knife and hides it before the teacher turns around. Phillip's friends high-five him for being so quick and sneaky. Phillip and his friends hang out in the nearby woods after school. Other kids hang there to watch Phillip and his friends practice throwing knives. They throw the knives at paper drawings of humans, which are tied to the trees. "Phillip's dad owns a collection of knives, so it must be okay that he spends his time doing this," Trish thinks.

When Trish gets home, her brother Sam is playing his favorite video game. It's the same game that was a favorite of the killers of the Columbine High School massacre in Colorado. The killers were kids who took out guns and killed their classmates. For every kill made in the game, the player is awarded with a high score. It teaches the player how to shoot a virtual gun in a very realistic fashion. "Sam is allowed to play his video games after he's done with schoolwork, so it mustn't be a bad influence, or Mom and Dad wouldn't allow him to play them," she reflects.

After dinner, Trish and her mother watch her mom's favorite show. It's a fictional show about doctors in the emergency room of a hospital. It's really realistic though, because it shows a lot of blood and details about surgery. The doctors occasionally fight and actually push or hit each other. Her mom calls it an intelligent soap opera. What her mom doesn't understand is that the show is sending a message that it's all right for responsible, intelligent adults to settle their arguments with physical violence. Her mom watches a lot of "intellectual soap operas," including detective shows where violence is a constant theme. "Mom loves this stuff, so it must be okay," Trish thinks.

Trish also watches sports with her dad. During the game the announcers praise the players for their rough game playing and displays of masculine strength. Commercials during the game breaks deliver the same kind of messages, such as that a guy is more masculine when he is physically assertive or aggressive, even if the purpose of the commercial is to sell shaving foam. Trish's dad tries to explain game strategies to Trish, but the overall lesson is that you have to be tough to be a man and to succeed.

Trish's day is not unlike that of any other U.S. child or teen. Across the United States, young people can count on being exposed to some form of human aggression throughout the day. The violence of the world is all around us, and its images are brought to us as news and entertainment in huge daily doses.

One of the main issues associated with violence is whether it's good for youth to be exposed to its images. Studies have shown that being exposed to large doses of violent images leads to desensitization. Desensitization causes us to react with less and less emotion the more that we are exposed to something. Desensitization happens to children, teens, and adults.

Studies regarding exposure to violent images and themes have shown that it causes us to become more desensitized toward human suffering. The studies also show because we are being desensitized, we are more likely to become aggressive and to react to life situations with aggressive, destructive reactions rather than rational, positive reactions.

Political leaders, educators, researchers, and parents are interested in understanding what the influence of violence and its images do to America's youth. They also hope to find ways of removing violent images from our society. In efforts to understand how to remove or control violence, we must examine what it is, how it's created, and how it has become a powerful influence in our society.

Many of us are also looking for ways of dealing with the violence that is present in our world today. This includes finding ways of avoiding the outbreak of violence and reacting to images and themes in nonviolent ways. This book will help you to understand violence, its images and themes in our society, and how to cope with its seemingly ever-present existence.

Mass Media
and Our Society

There have been societies in human history that existed without the influence of violence. There are nonviolent societies even today, including the Gebusi, Fore, and Arapesh of New Guinea; the Mbuti and Kung of Africa; and the Semai of Malaysia.

In nonviolent societies such as these, it takes effort on every member's part to make sure that violence is kept to a minimum. Members establish rules that promote and reward the act of sharing and nonviolent behavior. Each member of these societies practices and lives by these rules, and is introduced to the rules at an early age.

Researchers who have studied these nonviolent cultures—such as Ashley Montagu, E. Richard Sorenson, Colin Turnbull, and Patricia Draper—believe that violence is further prevented by all that is shown and taught to members during their youth. Adult members are seen as nonviolent role models who do not engage in aggressive behavior such as hitting, fighting, or verbally insulting another member. Youth are not physically punished, but are ignored or scolded for any inappropriate behavior.

In the event that a conflict does arise, members solve it though nonaggressive demonstrations and negotiations. Youth are taught that cooperation is the important fundamental of life, whereas youth in our culture are taught the importance of competition and to enjoy competing against others. Although some competition is good—as when it causes us to strive to be better people—many competitions bring out aggressive behavior in participants. These researchers believe that placing a major emphasis on competition and aggression is what contributes to the occurrence of violence in our society.

In hopes to minimize the occurrence of violence in our society, we have established social codes and laws. Social codes are rules of behavior that demonstrate how we would like to be treated by others. One of the most well known social codes is "Do unto others as you would have them do unto you," which dates back to the time of the New Testament. This means that if you would like to be treated kindly, then you should treat others kindly.

Laws are strict codes that are enforced by the government and its representatives. Laws are meant to protect us from hurting ourselves and one another. Our schools and workplaces also establish rules, which govern our behavior during attendance there.

Social codes, laws, and rules are abstract—they are not physical things. Violence, however, is not abstract—it has real-world effects such as injury, suffering, and death. In order to ensure that members of our society follow our laws, real-world consequences are established to punish members who break laws. The punishments include monetary fines, restrictions of civil liberties, imprisonment, and even death. Even with rigid laws and punishments, however, violence still exists. This is where the media becomes a controversial part of violence and our society.

What Is the Media?

The word *media* is used to encompass many forms of public communication and expression, such as newspapers, magazines, television, films, music, books, and computers. The media offers every member of our society the opportunity to communicate his or her ideas and issues. Companies and industries use all forms of media to communicate ideas and to inform, educate, entertain, and stimulate the public—while making a profit.

Many members of the media say that the violent images and themes we see, hear, and read about daily are used as a mirror to show everyone what is really going on in the world. This argument fails when violent images and themes are glorified in ways that create hype, demand, and profit. Even some news programs deliberately use misleading messages to boost ratings, many of them regarding the occurrence of violence.

Sarah watches the news with her parents. She feels good about knowing what is going on in the world. This knowledge gives her the ability to talk about a variety of topics with different people. The news is a source of education for Sarah, and for many other people.

"I've watched all kinds of news shows with my folks," she says. "They're all really different in the way that they present the news. Some have flashy graphics and music, while others have a newscaster and very little else. I used to like when the reports were accompanied by pictures that were flashed on the screen, especially pictures of car crashes. The sight of how an accident could mangle a car was interesting to me . . . until my brother Josh's accident.

"I was so happy for my brother. It was his senior prom, and he was a candidate for prom king. He had a great year and a cool girlfriend named Lise who I really liked," she continues. "Lise and I used to go shopping for gifts for my brother. My dad and stepmom trusted me in her care because she really had her act together. She, like my brother, was already registered at college, and the two of them were hoping to get married during their sophomore year.

"On prom night, my brother's best friend, Tom, his date, Julia, Lise, and Josh all went in the same car. My brother's friends said that at the prom, Josh and the three others had the time of their lives. I have pictures from the dance on my mirror and hung up in my room. Josh's smile was huge, as it used to get whenever he had a great time.

"After the dance my brother's group planned to go to a popular hangout that was in a farm field near school. The farm was abandoned, but there was a barn left standing that the high-schoolers hung out in. People were already partying there even before my brother's group left for the farm. Soon some of those kids were racing down the curvy road that led to and from the barn. Around one of the curves, my brother's car was approaching.

"The police came to our house around four in the morning. We weren't expecting Josh back until the next day because he was going to spend the night at Tom's house. The officer looked a little uncomfortable and she launched into a sentence that would change our lives forever, 'Your son Josh was killed instantly in an auto accident that occurred a few hours ago.'

"My Dad wanted to be taken to the scene of the accident, to understand what had happened, but the officer assured us that what needed to be done was to go to the morgue to be sure that it was indeed Josh. My stepmom, my dad, and I hoped that it wasn't Josh, and that maybe the police were mistaken. My parents left me in the waiting area outside the morgue doors in the care of the officer and went into the morgue. I heard my parents moan . . . I heard them sob. I didn't need to see what they were seeing to know that my brother was dead.

"On our way out, we saw the parents of Lise, Tom, and Julia. All of them had been asked to come identify the bodies. My brother's entire group was killed in the accident. An accident such as this, in our town, was big news. Over the next few hours, our yard became a parking lot for the media. One of my favorite newscasters even had the nerve to ring our doorbell to ask for comments. My parents and I were devastated. We wanted to be left alone to cope with our loss.

"Within hours, photographs of my brother's smashed car were broadcast on all of the channels.

There were also false reports that my brother had been drinking. No alcohol was found in his body during the autopsy. The first time I saw the photos, and saw them showing the blood from the scene of the accident, I threw up. I couldn't stomach the sight of how my brother had been killed, and I couldn't stand the fact that the world was being led to believe that my brother was drunk.

"For the first time, the random photographs of smashed cars had meaning beyond satisfying my curiosity or entertaining my interests. The photos meant that somewhere else, people like me were suffering. It took the death of my brother to help me understand that the pictures had consequences. That family members would feel anguish in their hearts every time they were exposed to the photos. For the first time, I wished never to see a car crash photo again.

"It's taken me years since Josh's death to watch the news without emotionally reacting to photos of car crashes. I like a particular news program that's known for its accuracy in reporting the facts. It also reports the news without using the graphic pictures associated with the stories. I realize that I don't need to see those pictures to understand the story, and that most news programs only air the graphic photos in hopes of beating out the competition in the ratings. They can keep their ratings, I don't need to see it to believe it."

Many of us live our entire lives without realizing what Sarah did. She is unlike many of us because when she turns on the television, she searches for its educational values first, and its entertainment values last. From her personal experience, Sarah learned that even news programs are guilty of releasing misinformation. She understands that the medium of television is not an exact science, and that even though something is broadcast, it doesn't mean that it's the whole story, or even a story of value.

She also understands that real human suffering is often abused and used as entertainment for television viewers. Above all, she knows that for every violent image or theme she sees, hears, or reads about, there are real-world consequences, and that someone related to those violent images and themes has suffered.

One of the most important skills in being able to cope with a media issue is to develop a well-informed opinion. When dealing with the media, we often forget that there are two sides to every story. The media shapes our reactions and makes us think that we are learning the only real side to the story. Sarah learned that behind every story, there are other truths left unsaid or even false reports that leak into the story—and that there are further consequences beyond what we are shown.

Does the Media Like Violence?

Violence is a learned behavior. We learn it from our families, our media, and our society. We learn about aggression—and how to express it—by watching others. We learn how to express our aggression through violence by imitating what we see or have seen others do.

A popular expression is "Violence begets more violence." This means that when violence occurs, more violence will most likely follow. If a person hits you, or is aggressive toward you, your reaction can be violent or nonviolent. According to the Senate report *Children, Violence, and the Media,* (a report on American youths between seventh and twelfth grades), we will most likely react to violence with violence if we are exposed to media violence on a regular basis.

If we know that the presence of violence can actually bring about more violence, then why do we show it? Why does violence exist as a part of our media? The answer is that more than at any other time in history, our society and the media are strongly intertwined with one another.

Members of society and members of the media look to each other for direction. The interests, likes, and dislikes of a society are shown through its media. At the same time, the interests, likes, and dislikes of a society are shaped by its media. Public interest can direct the media, and the media can direct public interest.

An example of the relationship between media and society is the popularity of aggressive reality shows such as *Cops.* The concept of the show is relatively new, since twenty years ago, few people would have been interested in watching shows starring real people instead of actors. *Cops* was presented to the public, and for the first time, the public was able to view the drama and violence of real-life police work as a main form of entertainment. The public acceptance and interest in real-life drama has allowed the media to produce and air many more reality-based drama shows.

The Popularity of Violence

Just as there are many forms of media, there are many forms of violence. From random acts of violence against innocent bystanders, to the organized violence of contact sports, we have access to it from the media if we are interested in it.

Horror movies, which can be extremely violent, are popular not only because the media creates a great deal of hype during promotions, but many of us actually like the feelings that come from being shocked or scared—in a safe setting. The media delivers what we want; horror movies use suspense and shocking images to thrill us. The violent images of horror movies are meant for entertainment purposes only—to scare or shock us in a safe setting. They aren't meant to be admired or repeated in real life.

In horror films and television shows, the actor isn't really dead, and the knives, guns, and murder devices aren't real weapons. But the reality is that for every violent act that you see in a fictional account, a human has actually done something similar—or worse—to another human in real life. During the span of time that you are sitting in the movie theater watching a horror film, someone in the real world is suffering because of violence.

Furthermore, studies on media practices show that films and programs will most likely not show you the reality of suffering that is caused by a violent act. Actors will clutch their wound and slump to the floor. In many violent projects the victim can receive a fatal blow, and yet somehow is able to run after or attack the attacker. In reality, the wounded person would be bleeding heavily and physically struggling to remain upright. If the wounded person is lucky, paramedics will come in time to help him or her. Families will be notified and there will be further suffering and pain while they watch their loved one suffer or die.

When faced with this knowledge, the sensationalized, hyped-up horror movie doesn't look so appealing. By thinking about the reality behind violent acts, we see the horror movie for what it is—a glorification of violence in order to stimulate and make a profit. If a horror film does relatively well at the box office, you will soon see sequels to it. Eventually, after public interest "dies" off, so will the villain of the series. Horror series such as *Nightmare on Elm Street* and *Halloween* have retired, and new horror series, such as *Scream* and *I Know What You Did Last Summer,* have taken their places.

If you must see the latest craze in horror movies, remember that the violence you see is not to be imitated in real life. The violence you see, were it to happen in real life instead of in the movies, would have terrible, lasting consequences.

Media As a Business

The media is where the real world and the imaginary world unite. It's where truths are sometimes bent, reality is apparently altered, and messages are sometimes shaped to mislead or to entice specific responses from society. Many, if not all of us, take cues from the media on ways to live, look, and behave; what to buy; and how to treat one another. Just as the media has a part in shaping our lives, we can shape the media with our choices of where we spend our money and time.

Increases in sales of products that are advertised through the media allow companies and industries to understand what we want more or less of. Ratings and ticket sales also reflect our wants and dislikes. Some members of the media rely on oversaturation of their messages to gain acceptance of ideas that originally were rejected. Media members know that the more a person is exposed to something, the more he or she will become used to it. This eventually leads to acceptance, and even support.

Companies, industries, and advertisers are forever experimenting with their overall products through the media. To turn a profit, they continually adapt their products to deliver whatever they believe the public wants. They also spend their resources making their ideas more acceptable to us, which also allows them to turn a profit. The media is able to use and reflect our interests, and to create new interests for us as well.

When the media finds something that society is interested in, a cascade effect occurs. An example of this would be a movie that did unusually well at the box office. Elements and themes from that popular movie, including violent elements and themes, are copied by television programs, advertisements, music, and the other forms of media. Similar projects will be released in hopes that they will make as much money as the original.

A direct example of this is the recent practice of adapting video games into movies. We have seen this happen with *Mortal Combat, Dungeons and Dragons, Super Mario Brothers,* and *Tomb Raider.* Another example is when popular books or television shows, such as the *Simpsons, South*

Park, The X Files, or *Star Trek* are made into video games, or movies.

An example of the media cascade in music is the copying of popular acts, such as Alanis Morrisette, into other forms of media. Morrisette has a unique sound and style. With acceptance of her sound in the music industry, other forms of media began using her sound and style to sell products. Radio and television advertisements for products such as automobiles and long-distance telephone service used her sound and style—not her directly, but vocal artists who could imitate her sound and style—to sell products.

In this way, the relationship between the media and society strengthens in a cycle-like pattern. The media provides an interest, and the interest becomes accepted by some part of general society. The media further develops the interest to be included in more forms of media. More forms reach more parts of society. Any member of society will be exposed to that interest through one or another form of media, eventually leading to acceptance. Acceptance provides further demand from the public for that interest.

The Media Controversy

The main controversy surrounding violence in the media and our society is that some members of the media use graphic, violent images and themes that are unnecessary and harmful. A story that has a mugging scene in it doesn't need to show a victim being stalked, struck, molested, degraded, or robbed. It can show that the mugging happened by having a character reflect on the event, or by

A Look at the First Amendment

The rights of every member of our society are protected under the Constitution of the United States. Brought into effect on March 4, 1789, the Constitution establishes the fundamental laws of the United States. The First Amendment and nine others are a part of the Constitution called the Bill of Rights. The creators of the Constitution demanded that part of it would define the rights of individuals, which led to the creation of the Bill of Rights.

Amendment I—*Congress shall make no law respecting an establishment of religion, or prohibiting the free exercise thereof; or abridging the freedom of speech, or of the press; or the right of the people peaceably to assemble, and to petition the Government for a redress of grievances.*

This amendment allows each U.S. citizen the ability to worship and practice his or her own religion, and to express or communicate his or her own opinions and beliefs without censorship. This means that people may express ideas—good or bad, healthy or unhealthy, helpful or harmful—without the government's interference or censorship.

using the classic film noir technique of alluding to the event without actually showing it. When something is alluded to, you are given the details of the event, but you are not shown the action—your imagination pieces things together. You still understand that a mugging is taking place, but you don't need the violent images.

Although you might think that it would be easy to stop violent images and themes from being used—especially if they are unnecessary and harmful—it's really a complicated issue. By attempting to deny these media members the ability to use violent images and themes, we would be depriving them of their fundamental rights.

Because of the constitutional protection of freedom of expression, we need to rely on one another's sense of common decency. This often fails when we deal with people who have little sense of common decency. Freedom of expression protects those who believe in the need for pornography, prejudice, sexism, hate, and violence—all of which harm other people and their rights.

Those media members who believe that violent themes—and other harmful themes—are a necessary part of our media simply believe that "if you don't like it, you can turn it off. Don't buy the magazine. Don't watch the movie. Don't buy the records."

Youth in the Controversy

According to the Center for Media Education, teens are especially bombarded by messages from the media. Young people are targets because they are still developing a sense of self. They have a strong desire to be accepted.

Members of the media are all too happy to show you how to be accepted, especially when you buy certain things, or act a certain way. You're at an age where you can sometimes be persuaded before you have had a chance to decide according to your own instincts and your own opinions. In fact, the media often tries to get to you before you form your own opinions about who you are, what you like, and what you need.

Because you are a media target, you need to protect yourself with the right attitude about bad influences. The influences that you are exposed to in your early and teen years play an important part in who you become. Studies have shown that both good and bad influences help us to become who we are as adults. The media is a place that is home to both good and bad influences.

You should know that there are members in the media who lack concern for your developmental needs. These members know of the harm that violent images do to youth, and still choose to aim their violent projects specifically toward you. Just last year, the United States Federal Trade Commission (FTC) studied the media industry practices in popular movies, music, and video games. The commission found that over 50 percent of these popular projects specifically marketed violence as a form of entertainment to youth.

According to FTC chairman Robert Pitofsky, the study uncovered the market plans of many media projects, and cited one such plan involving a studio's release of a movie. The movie was rated R—it is not meant for anyone under seventeen—and the studio's plan was "to find the elusive teen market and make sure everyone between the ages of twelve and eighteen was exposed to the film."

Your parents and teachers will try to shield you from the bad influences of certain images and themes, but the images and themes have a way of reaching their audience. It's up to you to decide how you are going to interpret these images and themes, and how they are going to affect you. Part of being able to protect yourself against bad influences is understanding what they are and knowing that they are unnecessary in your life.

What Is Violence in the Media?

During a single day of exposure to the U.S. media, a person could read about, hear about, and see several hundred violent images or themes. During the same exposure, a person could also see several images of humane acts, as well as images of love and kindness.

After witnessing a courageous act portrayed in the media, many people have been moved to do the same in their own lives. Could the same be true when witnessing the violence of the world through our media? Several studies and reports, including those conducted and reviewed by the U.S. Senate, the American Medical Association, the American Academy of Pediatrics, the American Academy of Child and Adolescent Psychiatry, and the National Institute of Mental Health, have shown that—without a doubt—the answer is yes. Violence in our media leads to real-world violence.

Beyond knowing that violence in the media really can shape our actions, we need to know exactly what makes a media message a violent one. Furthermore, we need to understand that violence in the media really is not necessary, as some members of the media argue it is. Also, we need to remember that there are several other factors, in addition to improper media use, that could lead a person down the path to violence. These factors include home life, a personal history of violence, and how a person copes with conflict.

Organizations Looking Out

In addition to our parents and teachers, there are many people who do care about the society that adults are making for you. Powerful organizations such as the American Academy of Child and Adolescent Psychiatry, and the National Institute of Mental Health work to protect you and your right to not be exposed to harmful influences.

These organizations have reviewed over 1,000 studies and research projects that have spanned the last forty years. Some of these studies include the Parents Television Council study, *Sex, Violence, and Foul Language on Prime Time Television;* the Mediascope study, *Media Television Violence;* the Surgeon General's office study, *Media Violence;* the U.S. Attorney General's Task Force study, *Family Violence;* and the Center for Communication and Social Policy's *National Television Violence Study.*

These studies and research projects were in-depth, some lasting for a period of three or more years. They focused on the effects of violence in television and movies. The organizations concluded that violence in these forms of media lead to real-world violence. Conclusions such as these have helped to establish strict rules and rating systems for television and film that can at least limit what media violence finds its way to you.

There are also several members of the media who purposely work to make the media a more youth-friendly place.

Writers and directors such as Gary Ross (*Pleasantville, Dave,* and *Big*) work to make their projects considerate of the needs of youth. Ross has publicly stated that for each project, he considers the effects that it will have on society, and on the youth who may see it. Steve Case, chairman of America Online, agrees on the importance of limiting young people's access to violent video games on the Internet.

People such as Ross and Case are responsible media members who know the real-world consequences of what is expressed through the media. They provide young people with quality programs, music, magazines, books, video games, and movies. Many of them urge other members of the media to be more responsible about what gets expressed publicly, especially through one of the most powerful forms of media—television.

Growing Up with the TV

Our society has made television one of the most important forms of media. According to psychologist and author Madeline Levine, the average U.S. household has a television set turned on for more than seven hours a day. We have also made it an important part of our lives from the time that we are young. Parents have used the television as a source of entertainment for their children for more than thirty years.

The idea of having a source of entertainment to occupy their children makes life easier for many parents. Toddlers show an immediate interest in the television set. Many toddlers mimic what they hear and see on television. Preschoolers become more interested in television as they grow. Although preschoolers pay close attention to television programming, they are not able to distinguish between commercials and shows, or fiction and reality.

As many children enter the school years, they make their own efforts to include television in their daily activities. They often want to stay up late to watch shows that are made for adults. Many youths between the ages of ten and seventeen spend most of their free time watching television or listening to music. More than half of the youth in the United States have television sets in their bedrooms. Youths raised on television are the least likely to read a book in their leisure time, according to several sources such as authors/researchers Kate Moody, John P. Murray, Barbara Lonnborg, and organizations such as Mediascope.

According to studies by organizations including the American Academy of Pediatrics and the National Institute of Mental Health, youths heavily influenced by television while they were growing up have certain mental and physical qualities in common. Studies have proven that youths who are heavy viewers are more likely to be aggressive, cynical or negative, less imaginative, and less capable students. According to Dr. Miriam Baron of the American Academy of Pediatrics, young people are more likely to weigh more if they are heavy television viewers. By the time an average American youth graduates high school, he or she will have spent considerably more time in front of the television set than in front of his or her teachers.

So what does television teach you? During prime-time television—the time that you would be watching in the evening—you will see from five to fifteen violent acts per hour. With the mere flip of the remote, you could also see interesting and educational documentaries about human achievements or excellence—you just have to look for them.

By the time that you graduate from high school you will have seen around 200,000 acts of violence—30,000 resulting in murder. The National Television Violence Study and the U.S. Senate concluded that television media violence teaches young people aggressive behaviors and attitudes, and that youth actually become fearful of being victimized by violence. Without proper coping skills, children and teens often react to fear with violence or aggression.

This means that you, members of your age group, or your younger brothers and sisters could fall victim to the cycle of media violence and fear. The way to combat fear is to become informed and to understand that the fear you are feeling about being victimized is a result of the influences around you. You can help ease your fear by talking about it with an informed adult—be it a parent, teacher, youth leader, or counselor.

Violent Images and Themes

Violence occurs on both mild and severe levels. Violence affects humans both physically and mentally. Violence takes place physically, or outwardly, in the form of a person causing pain that is felt by another person's body. Hitting, stabbing, shooting, and molestation are all forms of physical violence. Violence also takes place mentally, or inwardly, in the form of a person verbally attacking or manipulating another person. An abuse of this kind occurs in our thoughts and emotions. Name-calling and putting someone down through humor are acts of mental violence.

Images or themes of a violent nature are expressed in photographs, advertisements, films, music, television shows, commercials, books, magazines, sports, and video games. If an image or theme shows a person deliberately using force or weapons to do the following things, the image or theme can also be considered violent in nature:

⮑ Achieve a goal

⮑ Act out an instant angry impulse

⮑ Acquire material possessions

⮑ Defend against verbal or physical assault

⮑ Further a cause

⮑ Intimidate other human beings

⮑ Self-mutilation

⮑ Show aggression toward other human beings

⮑ Stop the actions of another human being

⮑ Torture or hold another human being captive

Ratings to Sort It Out

Perhaps you have noticed that at the start of many television programs there is a little white square with black letters flashed on the screen. These are ratings, which describe the show's contents. Programmers can air the ratings at the beginning of their shows to display what the content of the program is. Viewers then read the ratings to determine whether the program's content is suitable for them.

The process of using ratings is entirely voluntary. Programmers are not required to use the ratings if they don't want to. Entire networks, such as BET, have decided to ban the rating system from their networks altogether. They believe that the rating system is a form of censorship. Censorship is a process where parts of an original message are not communicated, or are altered, because they are believed to be harmful or unnecessary.

Other stations use the rating system as a courtesy to their viewers. They believe in allowing their viewers to make informed choices about what to watch. You can use these ratings to help you determine whether a show is going to waste your time with exploitative violence or be worth your time, enriching and educating your mind.

TV-Y   Designed for very young children.

TV-Y7 Designed for children seven years and older. There may be themes that are too mature for children younger than seven.

TV-G   Designed for all youth. It will contain little or no violence or aggressive behaviors.

TV-PG Will contain themes and images that will best be viewed with the help of a parent or adult. Adults will be able to explain any images or themes that involve violence or mature matters.

TV-14 Considered unacceptable for any youth under the age of fourteen. It's also best viewed with a parent or adult to help discuss the images and themes that you will see during viewing.

TV-MA Meant for adults only. Not only will it contain violence and controversial themes, but it will not have dialogue or content that an average youth will find desirable.

"We did a project in school that really woke me up," said Dimitri, fifteen years old. *"My teacher asked us to spend time outside of school studying media violence. We did two different exercises. The first exercise was to go through magazines and pull out pictures or things that seemed violent. We were to describe how they made us feel, and to discuss any questions that we had about media violence.*

"I started looking through my dad's National Geographic. *I paged though and couldn't find anything that I thought was violent. Then I looked through my rock and rap magazines. I found several images that showed people acting aggressively toward one another. The violent images were both in the advertisements and in the sections where they showed clothing, interviews, or music artists.*

"Show-and-tell was really interesting. The images that my classmates brought ranged from photos of weapons and blood to a picture of a woman being held by a muscular man. I had a hard time understanding how the picture of the woman and man could be violent . . . until discussion time.

"My teacher pointed out that the woman in the photo wasn't smiling, which suggested that the experience was not pleasant for the woman. She also pointed out

that the man holding the woman was very physically strong, which might suggest to boys that if they are big and strong they can hold or do anything they want. My teacher went on to explain that it was subtly violent because the picture suggested that a man's strength can hold a woman captive.

"I had seen that same picture before and didn't consider it violent. Now I looked at the woman's expression and realized that her face was emotionless. And the guy was flexing all of his muscles as if he needed to restrain her movement. Suddenly, I realized that powerful messages aren't always obvious. They can sneak up on you if you don't know how to evaluate them properly.

"My teacher taught us to look at ads and images and to ask ourselves, 'What does this image have to do with the written message? Are the words filled with aggressive adjectives like destroy, dominate, and beat? Does the image really have to do with the purpose of the ad or story?' I realized that images were also about influencing me in ways that I wasn't aware of.

"The second exercise was cool, too. We kept a notebook with us over the week and wrote down every time we were exposed to violence. The first day I wrote about stuff that I saw on television. Most of it came from the cop shows that my Dad watches. The rest of it came from the music video channel.

"After discussing my examples, my teacher asked me if I played any video games or watched cartoons as well. I said, 'Sure, every day.' She smiled and said, 'Well Dimitri, although this is a good start, you might *have missed some.' Everybody else had only a few examples, too. She asked all of us to spend the next evening really on the lookout for violence.*

"Sure enough, the next day we each had a bunch of examples. She asked us to spend the next evening focusing on one media violence example. She asked us to really think about what the motivation was behind the violent action. She also asked us to decide if it was a hero or a villain doing the violence. Lastly, we were to give examples of what happens in real life after our example might occur.

"I chose a scene from the cartoon The Simpsons. *Krusty the Clown and Homer get a violin back from some Mafia members. There is a shoot-out and one of the members gets shot. When asked where on his body he was shot, the character says, 'Suck a lemon.'*

"During discussion, I answered the questions that my teacher asked us to think about when interpreting the scenes. The violent action happened because the members were using guns to shoot at each other, and it was supposed to be funny that one of the members got shot. The Mafia members, who had the violin, were the villains. In real life, had he been shot, I think that he would have been screaming in pain, and probably bleeding all over the place. I doubt that he would be so casual about being shot.

"It was a great exercise. We learned that there aren't a lot of violent images and themes that show what would really happen to the characters in real life. People get stabbed, shot, hit, and slapped in the media and they barely react. Even a pinch on my

arm is enough to make me react with an 'Ouch!' and I have to rub the area of skin until it feels better.

"It's been a few weeks since the exercises. I see the media differently now. Now I know that what's shown to me isn't the whole picture, and that there is a lot more that happens in real life than what the media shows. I also see that a lot of media forms use violence even when there are other ways of dealing with the situation. Some even use violence as a source of humor."

Allowing Yourself Control of Media Violence

Dimitri learned that violence isn't always obvious. In addition to the things that Dimitri learned about violence, we need to ask ourselves if there are other alternatives to the violence that we see. If one show has a heavy emphasis on violence, is there something else that you could be watching . . . or doing?

Ask yourself the following questions when you are watching, reading, looking at, and listening to programs with violent themes and images:

⮑ Are the characters violent or aggressive to begin with?

⮑ Is this sending me mixed messages?

⮑ Is the violence made to appear humorous, does it have a macho quality or seem exciting?

⮑ Are any problems solved without violence?

31

➪ Do those involved as victims show the suffering and pain that the violence causes?

➪ Is there anything actually educational or informative about it?

If you think about these items while you are watching, reading, looking at, and listening to projects with violent themes and images, you will learn how to be a discerning viewer. Being a discerning viewer means that you take an active interest in the things that you are shown and exposed to.

Anytime that a project has violent characters—characters that use violence to achieve goals—you are watching something that is promoting violence. If the program tells you that violence is wrong, but has a character who solves his or her problems through violence, it's sending you mixed messages. If the story's violence is portrayed in a way that is humorous, sensationalized, or hip—it's promoting ideas that can lead to unhealthy attitudes and behaviors toward yourself and others.

As a discerning viewer, you become the person in charge of your own media watching. You can look for programs that will teach you how to react to real-world problems without aggression or violent behavior. You should look for stories that solve problems without violence. They will help you learn about positive solutions to the problems of the world around you.

If a program does show violent themes or images, does it show what happens as a consequence of the violence? Stories like these will at least show you that there

Signs of Media Violence Influence

According to the American Psychological Association and the American Academy of Pediatrics, there are signs or symptoms that can tell you if you, a friend, or a sibling is suffering from the effects of media violence. In the event that you know someone who is exhibiting the following behaviors, which are symptoms of media violence influence, tell a parent or teacher. A youth suffering from the effects of media violence will exhibit any or all of the following behaviors:

➷ Does not listen to authority figures regularly

➷ Does not respect the feelings or rights of others

➷ Mistreats others

➷ Relies on physical violence or threats of violence to solve conflicts

➷ Often expresses the view that life is unfair or unkind

➷ Does poorly in school, skips class, or misses school for no apparent reason

➷ Gets into trouble at school, or drops out entirely

➷ Joins a gang

➷ Gets involved in fighting, stealing, or destroying property

➷ Drinks alcohol and/or uses inhalants or drugs

is pain and suffering involved in every act of violence. Many programs with violent images and themes leave off at the event of the violent act, without showing you what happens as a result of the violence. This is what many researchers at organizations such as Mediascope and the American Academy of Pediatrics believe leads us to lose touch with reality when dealing with violence.

Getting Exposed to Media Violence

Many violent images and themes in the media are used for a purpose, whether to promote an idea, sell a product, film, or program, or show us what is going on in the world. Many supporters of violence in the media feel that it's a valuable teaching tool for young people. They believe that there is good media violence and bad media violence.

Good and Bad Violence

Some supporters of violence in the media, such as media analyst Dr. Jean Killbourne, feel that there is such a thing as appropriate violence for youth. Dr. Killbourne states that appropriate use of media violence is that which shows violence as harmful and bad, and that it's wrong to solve problems with aggression. Furthermore, some of these supporters believe that knowledge of real-world violence and of what people are capable of helps youths to be well-adjusted to today's world. Being well-adjusted means that you have the full ability to react to the world and its problems in healthy, constructive ways.

Organizations such as Mediascope and the American Academy of Pediatrics state that if violence is part of a youth project, showing the consequences of the violence is far more important that showing violence itself. According to their studies, if you are aware of the consequences of violence, you are less likely to behave in violent ways. Presently, according to the *National Television Violence Study,* over half of the media projects aimed for youth contain some level of violence. Unfortunately, more than 70 percent of these projects do not show the consequences of the violence. More than half of all victims in these projects are not shown to be experiencing pain as a result of the violence.

If there is appropriate media violence, we cannot measure how many violent images and themes would really be necessary to be considered a "good" amount. We also do not have direct proof that people of your age group with full knowledge of the world's violence actually do respond to life's conflicts in well-adjusted ways.

Another dilemma is: How do we expose youths to violent images without having desensitization occur? Reports from the U.S. Senate and Mediascope find that constant exposure to violent images and themes does lead to desensitization in viewers of all ages. When a person is desensitized, he or she is not a well-adjusted member of society. If a person were suffering, a well-adjusted person would react with concern and compassion, while a desensitized person would have little compassion or concern, and might not react at all.

Exposure

Whether sensationalized and unnecessary or for a supposedly good and useful purpose, the media exposes us to all forms of violence from the time that we wake up to the time that we go to bed. Television, music, computers, video games, magazines, books, and film all give us constant access to violent themes and images.

Many of these themes and images translate into real-world violence, especially among young people. According to Las Vegas detectives, in June of 1997 teenager Jeremy Strohmeyer sexually assaulted and murdered a seven-year-old girl in a Nevada casino. Jeremy told the detectives that the way he killed the girl was from a scene that he had watched on television. When the police investigated his home life, they discovered that Jeremy possessed and regularly used hundreds of Internet pictures containing child pornography and adult pornography of a violent nature as a source of entertainment. Many of us are aware of the effects of media violence; in fact, surveys published by Mediascope show that more than 70 percent of us believe that television and films are at least partly responsible for crimes committed by youth.

A CNN/*Time* magazine survey conducted with thirteen- to seventeen-year-olds showed that teens believe that the media is partly responsible for real-world youth violence. Of the teens surveyed, 75 percent said that the Internet is partly responsible for youth violence; 66 percent said that violence on television, films, and music is responsible; and 56 percent felt that violent video games are also to blame for youth violence. The U.S. Senate report *Children, Violence, and the*

Media states that television is directly responsible for 10 percent of the youth violence that occurs.

You don't have to be part of the violence. You can control what influences you. You and your friends can make your world fun without relying on unnecessary violence and aggression. The more control that you give yourself over the influence of violence, the healthier your outlook will be when faced with life's challenges.

Instead of reacting to challenges with the everyday violence that is around you, you can rely on your intelligence, instinct, and imagination—three things that are much more constructive and powerful than violence and aggression. Everyday people who use nonviolent methods instead of aggression in conflicts should be—and are—heroes or excellent role models. We can look to historical nonviolent heroes, such as Mohandas Gandhi, to learn how to react to conflict by using intellect, instinct, and imagination rather than violence. Gandhi, through nonviolent means, was able to play a major role in liberating India from Great Britain's powerful domination.

You can develop these characteristics by investing time and concern in yourself. This investment starts when you control what influences you. Know where you get exposed to violence and decide to look for another alternative that enriches rather than wastes your true abilities. Instead of watching a show with violent characters, or one that glorifies violence, which teaches you violent tendencies, try to watch a show about solving conflict through nonviolence. Stories about nonviolent characters can teach you how blatant aggression can be overcome through intelligent communication and nonviolent reactions.

If you are watching a program with realistically violent scenes, make certain that it continues through to show you realistic consequences, such as punishment, suffering, and permanent life-altering circumstances. While watching the program, ask yourself how you would have solved the conflicts without violence or aggression.

Television and Film

You turn on the television, sit back, and flip through the channels. You can find entire channels dedicated to action-packed, violent programming. At the same time, you can find channels that are dedicated to helping you enrich your mind through interesting, informative programming ranging from documentaries to thought-provoking series. You really do decide what you get exposed to when you hold the remote. The same is true for the movies that you decide to go see or rent.

A great deal of effort goes into advertising for movies and television shows. The advertisements for movies show as much action and hype as possible. They try to entice you into the theaters to see a movie that will keep you on the edge of your seat, while also trying to tell you that by not seeing the movie, you will miss out on something everyone else is enjoying.

A person who feels as if he or she is missing out on something will most likely jump at the chance to get in on it. For the film industry, this works like a charm. Many of us spend our time and money seeing movies that weren't anything like they were advertised to be. It's all part of the media's campaign to get us into the theaters. A movie is billed in as many ways as possible to be attractive to each one of us in one way or another. The same is true for television programs.

According to *Children, Violence, and the Media,* the average seventh grader watches around four hours of television a day. Imagine all of the things that you could learn in four hours of watching informative, entertaining programming instead of wasting your time watching repetitive, unnecessary violence—which teaches you nothing but how to behave violently. Furthermore, studies such as *Essential Information's Statistics on Television's Impact* and *Television's Impact on Health,* show that watching television is addictive.

Addiction occurs when we become dependent on something that we could otherwise live without. Try spending one day without watching television. The more difficult it is to do, the more likely that you are addicted. If you are addicted, chances are that you are watching too much television, while doing less of the other things that someone your age should be doing. Play sports, go out with friends, read, find a hobby, pick a subject in school that you would like to ace and make it a priority—just do something besides watching television.

Music

Think about when you hear a song for the first time. It's unfamiliar. You might even think that there's nothing special about it. The media knows, however, that if you hear it enough times, the song will become catchy to you, even if your first reaction was "Blechh!" This effect is even stronger if you happen to like the artist who puts out the songs.

Music truly stirs the soul; it can affect our moods. You probably have a favorite song that makes you happy, maybe another song that makes you want to rock out, and yet another one that makes you sad. Music is really a great communicator of human emotion. But there are also bad influences in music. Lyrics that urge you to do violent things are bad influences. Lyrics that glorify violence, or try to tell you that violence is cool are also bad influences.

According to the Parents Music Resource Center, the average teenager during the years between seventh and twelfth grade listens to more than 10,000 hours of music. Teens who are fourteen to sixteen years old listen to music more than thirty-five hours a week. More than six of those hours are spent "listening" to music while watching music videos.

The Center for Media and Public Affairs did a study on nearly 200 music videos, and found nearly 2,000 acts of violence. Of the violence in these videos, close to one-third was extremely violent or very serious in nature. Not only might the lyrics be violent, but through watching the videos you are being forced to associate visual violent acts with the music. According to studies published by Mediascope, in music videos with violent images, men are three times more likely to be the aggressors, and white females are most frequently the victims.

Although research into the connection between violent videos and youth violence is freshly underway, one study, named the *Reduction of Aggressive Behavior After Removal of Music Television,* has already reported that teenagers in a locked treatment facility became less violent when the viewing of MTV was no longer allowed.

Particular musical styles, especially rap, can also affect youth behavior. Studies, which include Rehman and Reilly's *Music Videos: A New Dimension of Televised*

Violence, have found that heavy listening to rap music tends to make young people more accepting of violence and violent behavior. With rap music, violence doesn't end with the lyrics and videos; many rap artists have been charged with or arrested for violent acts in real life, some as serious as murder.

Some of these artists include Tupac Shakur, Eminem, and Sean Puffy Combs. Other celebrities, including actors and athletes, have been charged or arrested for the same reasons. They include Dennis Rodman, Carmen Elektra, figure skater Tonya Harding, football player Rae Carruth, O. J. Simpson, members of the band Everclear, and actor Wallace Langham.

If you are going to spend as many as five hours a day listening to music, make certain that it really enriches what you are about. Seek out music that inspires you to be creative and productive rather than destructive. If music plays a big part in your life, try to learn how to play an instrument, or to write your own music. Your love for music shouldn't turn you into someone who would hurt yourself or someone else.

"I was really into grunge music," says Trini, eighteen years old. "My first boyfriend, Kevin, and I went to see local acts every weekend. In fact, that's where I met Kevin. I noticed that he really loved the mosh pit, so I decided to go into it, too. The mosh pit is where you can freak out and slam yourself against other people. Kevin thought that I was cool for being the only girl tough enough to go into the pit, and he asked me out.

"My friends liked grunge music too, but they didn't like the mosh pits. They thought that I was crazy for

getting into something that could hurt me, but I felt powerful. It took me a long time to get it right without getting too banged up. One time, someone punched me in the nose, and I had a bruise for two weeks. I lied to my parents and told them that it happened during a volleyball game. I thought that it was cool that people thought I was tough. It was also cool to feel as tough as the guys. I'd hide my bruises from my parents. It was my little secret.

"Kevin started listening to heavy metal music, too. I tried to get into it, but I didn't like it as much as I liked grunge. Pretty soon Kevin started hanging out with the kids who went to metal shows instead of going to grunge shows with me. We began disagreeing more, and Kevin stopped hanging out. We had a big fight about it. At one point in the fight, he hit me. I couldn't forgive him for that. He asked how him hitting me was any different from what I let other people do to me in the mosh pits. He said that I liked aggression.

"I didn't have any answers for that. I really don't know why I did it, except that I saw other people doing it. Nobody explained to me what it meant besides the fact that we were letting off steam. It was our way of dealing with the pressures of being teens. Nobody told me that doing it might give other people the impression that I didn't care about myself. All the grunge videos on television showed big mosh pits, it just seemed like the thing to do.

"I did know for sure that Kevin hitting me was wrong. But the fact that I allowed others to hit me or to be physically aggressive toward me confused us both. I can't say that I was doing it for the music, because I

could just as well have listened to it from the audience instead of in the pit. I got swept up, and didn't think of the consequences. I made the choice, and it made me lie to my parents and hurt my body. It also gave Kevin the impression that I liked being abused.

"My parents were relieved when Kevin and I broke up. They said that they didn't like the way that I had been acting. They said that I seemed aggressive and moody during the time that we were together. They were right. I felt bad for lying to my parents, and for hurting myself in the pits. My parents had started to represent the guilt that I felt, the guilt that I wanted to forget. I had turned away from them, the last people that would ever want to hurt me. I had dealt with it by being more aggressive and moody, because I had no real idea of what I was doing, or what I should be doing. I was just doing what was out there, and what everybody else seemed to be doing."

Video Games and Computers

Computers have become a valuable source of education, information, and entertainment. Computers, the Internet, and video games have also become a favorite pastime of many children, teens, and adults. *Children, Violence, and the Media* states that out of every ten households with youths, seven have computers. Nearly half of those households have computers that are hooked up to the Internet.

The Senate report also shows that the amount of money spent every year on computer video games in the United States is more than $10 billion. That is almost double the amount of money that we spend on going to movie theaters. Generally, young people who own video games play them around an hour and a half each day.

The most commonly bought video games contain violent images and themes. According to sources such as Mediascope and the U.S. Senate report, out of every 100 youth, over half prefer to play games in the categories of fantasy or human violence. Only a small number—less than twenty—would chose educational games. The preference for violent video games over educational games grows out of constant hype, advertisements, and gimmicks.

Video games and the Internet have a similar effect to that of television and film. Some researchers, such as Dr. Brian Stonehill and Mark Weitzman, say that because video games are interactive, they are even more dangerous to us than the violent images on television and screen. They believe that because the violent acts are carried out by players, violent tendencies and urges are being developed. Violent video games teach and reward players for being skilled at killing and attacking.

Advertisements for video games use violence as a selling point. Video games compete with each other in the areas of realism, extreme violence, and graphics. Games rated for adults are sometimes pushed on teen markets. One extremely violent game, *Resident Evil 2,* was advertised in the magazine *Sports Illustrated for Kids,* which is a magazine that is published for young people. Even with a rating system for video games, the National Institute on Media and the Family found that only about 20 percent of retail and rental stores actually prohibit renting and selling

Becoming an Activist Against Hate and Violence

You can make the world a better place by reporting harmful sites to advocacy groups and your local police. A harmful Web site or chat group contains the following material:

- Child pornography

- Promotion or suggestions of killing or harming others

- Promotion of hate crimes

- Member harassment or stalking

- Adults that try to lure you into meeting them in person

- Illegal activities or promotion of illegal activities such as hacking, bomb making, terrorism, or weapon trading

To report Web sites or chat rooms that contain harmful elements such as these, write down the Web address, e-mail address, or name of the newsgroup involved, and the date that you came across it. Send this information to your local police and to your internet service provider (ISP). You can also report this information to safe Web advocacy organizations such as CyberAngels at www.cyberangels.org or Connect for Kids at www.connectforkids.org. These organizations will forward the information to the proper authorities. By doing something this simple, you will have become an activist against violence and hate.

adult games to children and minors. Some store clerks will even recommend violent games to minors to make the sale. One such instance is cited by the U.S. Senate Commerce Committee, which heard testimony about a twelve-year-old boy who bought an adult-rated video game at a Washington, D.C. video store at the recommendation of the store clerk.

According to sources such as Mediascope, the Media Awareness Network, and the U.S. Senate report, the Internet presents us with well over 1,000 Web sites that support hate, prejudice, and violence. These Web sites contain violent words, images, and music. You might wonder why such things exist as a part of our culture, but again, the right to publish these Web sites is protected by the First Amendment. Some sites even offer altered versions of popular video games that promote the individual site's values.

One such site offers an altered version of the game *Doom* that promotes racial violence and hatred. Several sites can be found that promote violent acts against people of other ethnic origins, women, and youth. If you stumble across one of these Web sites while surfing, remember that creators of these Web sites promote ideas that are destructive to our society. Rather than dedicating their energies to promoting values that are constructive, they promote violence and hatred. These are two things that damage our quality of life.

If you are going to spend your time with computers and video games, try to use programs and games that aren't violence-laden. The World Wide Web is a wonderful invention that should be used in ways that add to what you know about the world and life. Although you can find many sites about hate, aggression, sexual dysfunction, and violence, there are millions of more interesting, constructive subjects to learn about, all of which can be found on the Web. A simple word search on a subject such as asteroids, at sites such as Discovery.com or Britannica.com, can lead you into a world of fun discovery and limitless knowledge.

Magazines, Books, and Newspapers

Books, magazines, and newspapers occupy the part of our time that is not already occupied by work, school, hobbies, television, computers, and music. Sometimes the print media takes a backseat to those other diversions. Yet in every home, doctor's or dentist's office, hair salon and waiting room, an array of magazines and newspapers can be found.

Literary media is great because it's portable and offers in-depth coverage of a variety of interests and subjects. Magazines and books are published for nearly every interest. Newspapers, books, and magazines are great because you can always pick up from where you left off. You can also choose from a variety of topics and articles to read about, focusing on some and skipping others. Photographs and illustrations in magazines, books, and newspapers also help us to understand a topic or story in more detail.

Magazines and newspapers can be of a nonviolent nature, but still have violent images or themes in their advertisement pages. Companies and advertisement agencies are responsible for the ads' contents, but the managing members of the magazines and newspapers make the final decision on whether or not to run an advertisement—especially one that might endorse violent and offensive ideas. Magazines and newspapers can also have violent images or themes in their editorial section, which is the non-advertisement section.

Just as many adults have successfully requested that editors and publishers pull offensive advertising out of their magazines and newspapers, you can do the same. You can write a letter to the magazine or newspaper requesting to have violent and offensive images pulled from publication. If the questionable material is an advertisement, you can also write directly to the company that makes the product. You can strengthen your effort by having other people sign the letter as a show of public support for removal of the material.

There are a number of terrific magazines that bring you the issues of the world, without the unnecessary violence. This allows you to explore a topic without needless gimmicks. Magazines geared specifically for teens take your needs into consideration, and present information to you without unnecessary editorial or advertisement violence. Some magazines for youths about video games and toys do have a great number of violent images and themes, both inside and on the covers. Again, this is done in hopes that you buy that magazine instead of another.

If you spend some of your extra time reading, choose what you're going to read carefully. There are magazines that can keep your interest without gimmicks; you just have to look for them. Good reading books and materials have an informative tone and don't preach or suggest any-thing other than the relevant facts. If you're into fiction, try to read books that spark your imagination with new and interesting—rather than violent—images and ideas.

Effects of
Media Violence

Violent images and themes alone cannot make a person commit a violent act. There are many other factors that must combine for violence to happen. A person's family situation and upbringing, behavioral habits, past experiences with violence, and mental attitude are some of the factors that combine with the influence of media violence to cause a person to commit a violent act.

What can be controlled—with effort on everyone's part—is the amount of influence that media violence has over our lives. The less media violence there is in our lives, the less likely we are to commit violent acts. Research reviewed by the American Medical Association, the American Academy of Pediatrics, the American Academy of Child and Adolescent Psychiatry, and the National Institute of Mental Health has shown that there are three major effects from viewing media violence.

Any viewer of media violence can:

➝ Become knowledgeable about aggressive attitudes and behaviors

➝ Become desensitized to violence and the suffering that it causes in the real world

51

↩ Become paranoid around other people because of a fear of being victimized.

According to the *National Television Violence Study,* there are nine factors that play an important part in the harmful effects of media violence on viewers. How the nine factors are used in a project plays a role in the influence that media violence has over us and our actions.

The Violent Agent

The violent agent, or the person or thing committing the violent action, has a great effect on the way that violence influences us. If the agent is likeable, a person might try to do the same violent act to imitate the likeable character. Various studies published by Mediascope have shown that people are more likely to act aggressively after watching or seeing a hero-like character commit a violent act than after seeing a villain do the same act. In more than three-fourths of the violent images or themes, adult white males are the violent agent. Close to half of these men are made to have likeable qualities.

The Receiver or Victim

If the receiver of the violence is portrayed as negative or a character deserving of punishment, the viewer may believe that violence is a justified reaction to conflict. If the victim is portrayed as a likeable character, the viewer may experience fear and anxiety as a result of thinking that the same thing could happen to him or her. More than one-third of the victims in violent themes or images possess likeable qualities; nearly another one-third are not likeable, or negative.

Motivation

The motivation behind the violence plays a role in how we react to it. Violent images or themes are most often portrayed as being motivated by the need for personal gain, protection of life, or expression of anger. Aggressive tendencies are reduced when the violence is viewed as unjustified. If an innocent bystander is brutally attacked, the viewer will be less likely to want to repeat the violence. If someone is attacked who is deemed to be a negative character, the viewer is more likely to repeat the violent act.

Weapon

The visual effect of weapons can evoke aggressive thoughts and behaviors in viewers. In real life, viewers might become confused by the presence of a weapon, such as a police officer's gun, seeing it as a violent situation, even if it's not being used. More than a quarter of all violent images or themes include the use of a gun.

Overexposure

The amount of violence to which a person is exposed can lead to a numbing effect on the viewer's emotions, or desensitization. As a result of desensitization, the viewer will lack sympathy and concern for the welfare of others. This can lead to an acceptance of violence as a problem-solving alternative. More than half of all violent images and themes portray repeated violent acts against the same victim by the violent agent.

Realism

The more realistic a violent theme or image is, the more likely that the viewer will think aggressive thoughts or behave in an aggressive manner. More than half of all violent images and themes take place in real-world settings, such as a school, workplace, or home.

Reward or Punishment

When the agent is punished for his or her violent act, viewers are less likely to become aggressive. When the agent is rewarded for a violent act, viewers are more likely to become aggressive. However, in more than half of the violent images or themes, violence is neither rewarded or punished.

Realistic Consequences

When there are images or themes of pain and suffering that accompany the violence, viewers are less likely to become aggressive. Aggressive tendencies are increased, however, when there are no consequences shown as a result of a violent act. In more than half of the violent images or themes, no pain, suffering, or consequences are shown.

Humor

When violent images or themes are combined with humor, the viewer's understanding of real consequences is minimized. A viewer is more likely to become aggressive when violence is lightened by humor. Almost one-half of all violent images or themes contain humor as well.

Discussing Violence

In addition to these factors, whether the viewer discusses the violent image or theme with a parent or adult also makes a difference in the effects of media violence. When young people discuss violence with an adult, they are often shown a perspective that they wouldn't normally develop on their own. Adults and parents can help you by explaining the real-world consequences of violence, and by discussing other possible alternatives to what you saw or heard.

Violent images and themes should not be confused with the natural conflict that occurs in life. When two people have conflicting viewpoints, a confrontational situation will often arise. Watching or being exposed to natural conflict can help teens understand the importance of choosing peaceful alternatives. Understanding conflict also allows you to develop important negotiating skills that can help you to avoid aggressive behaviors and situations.

Discussing conflict with an adult or parent can also help you to further understand the difference between a violent theme and a theme that contains conflict. It will also help you to sort out the difference between realistic images and reality.

"I think that my younger brothers and I came from a pretty average family. My parents are okay; they don't fight as much as other kids' parents do. My life is all right; I play in sports at school and am part of the school band. My brothers and I were always pretty typical kids, messing around after school, playing games with the other kids on the block. Pretty all-American, that's us.

"A lot of our family time was spent in front of the television. We'd watch all kinds of shows, ranging from educational shows like Nova, *to funny shows like* Beavis and Butthead. *My father's favorite sport was football. He really used to get into it. He even had a*

foam football that he tossed with my brothers during commercials. He loved the teams that play with gusto. Mom loves cooking shows; she even has a little television set in the kitchen.

"My brothers, Tosh and Ryan, started watching professional wrestling. Their favorite wrestlers were Stone Cold Steve Austin and The Undertaker. For Halloween, Tosh, who was six years old, dressed as The Undertaker. When the World Wrestling Federation came to town, Dad took my brothers to see it.

"Some of the older kids on the block had wrestling matches in one of the backyards every Saturday. The parents who owned the house went on trips every weekend, so the house was left in charge of Stanley, a sixteen-year-old. We would go over and watch the matches. It looked real, and some kids got hurt, but most of the things that they were doing were staged. Stanley was really cool; we liked that he let us hang out to watch the matches.

"One of the weekends, I didn't go over with Tosh and Ryan; I stayed home. About the middle of the afternoon, I heard an ambulance siren coming closer and closer. I looked out the window and saw that it had stopped four houses down . . . at Stanley's. I ran down the street to find out what had happened.

"In front of Stanley's house, Ryan stood with his mouth open. 'I didn't mean it, please don't tell Mom and Dad,' he said. I don't know how long he had been standing there, but he had dried blood on his hands and shirt. I tried to get to the backyard, but there were too many people standing around. Ryan slowly stumbled back toward our house.

"I snuck into the front door of Stanley's house and ran to the back door where I could see the backyard. The paramedics were bent over someone lying down. I recognized Tosh's leg sticking out from the huddle. A shot of shock went through my whole body, I felt my heart skip a beat. I could glimpse little sights of Tosh face while the paramedics scrambled around him. His face was bloody and he wasn't moving. The paramedics carefully put him on a stretcher and went around the side of the house to the front.

"I looked for Stanley but he wasn't to be seen. I kept asking everybody for him, but one of his best friends, named David, said that he ran off after Tosh got hurt. David explained that Tosh and Ryan were tag-team wrestling on teams against each other. At one point, Ryan did a move that Tosh and he used to do in our living room. They would run toward each other, pushing each other over by hitting each other around the shoulders and chest. They never did it for real, but this time Ryan had accidentally struck Tosh in the neck, which sent Tosh flying backwards. David said that blood came out of Tosh's mouth, and that Tosh couldn't breathe.

"By now my parents were at the ambulance, scream-ing for Tosh. The paramedics told my dad that Tosh wasn't breathing and that we needed to follow them to the hospital. They said that there wasn't room for fam-ily on the ambulance because Tosh needed emergency treatment. My mom, dad, Ryan, and I climbed into our car, and sped towards the hospital. My hands were shaking. My dad kept asking 'What happened?' Ryan couldn't answer, so I told my parents what had been

going on at Stanley's every weekend. My parents looked at each other, without saying a word.

"We arrived at the emergency room to be told by hospital staff to wait in a room. About five minutes passed, which seemed like an eternity. I kept thinking that Tosh would be fine. 'No one really gets seriously hurt on the wrestling shows. He'll be fine,' I told myself. Finally, the doctor came out.

"She asked to speak to my parents in the hall. I heard what she said. She said that Tosh was dead. She said that they tried to save him, but that his neck was broken and that they got to him too late.

"It's been three years since Tosh died. Ryan has had such a hard time with things. My parents don't blame him, but he blames himself. I don't know who to blame. I think that maybe if I was with them, it wouldn't have happened, but I can't be so sure. I remember thinking that it would be cool to join in the matches myself, but being a girl, I kept out of the matches. I can't blame Tosh or Ryan, they were just trying to have fun.

"My parents changed after the accident. We don't watch things that are violent anymore. Dad doesn't even watch football. He says that maybe he gave us the wrong idea about doing what we see on television. Mom still watches her cooking shows, and sometimes we just sit and watch them with her. I miss Tosh. I miss his smile and his laughter.

"It hurts to see Ryan so alone. He misses his little buddy so much. I hear him cry in his room sometimes. I know that if he had known that it was so dangerous, he and Tosh would have found something else *to do. Ryan wishes more than anything that on that Saturday, they were doing something else. Just that one day he wants back to make things right, which will never, ever happen."*

—*Molly, fifteen years old.*

What happened to Tosh was a result of what is called copycat violence. Parts of this scenario were taken from an account of something that actually happened in Dallas in May 1999. A seven-year-old boy accidentally killed his younger brother while imitating a wrestling move that he had seen on television. He demonstrated to police what he had done to his brother by using a doll.

Although some of us might say "Oh, I would never do that. He must have been out of his mind," the truth is that the boy wasn't out of his mind; he wasn't stupid. He was doing what all of us do, we imitate what we see, what we like, and what we are told we should like. Furthermore, his household wasn't a place where discussions about real consequences took place, and it was a household where the television set was the main source for entertainment.

Copycat Violence

According to the organization Mediascope, there are some documented cases of real-life violence that were inspired by violent images and themes in film, television, music, reading materials, video games, and the Internet. Research is just beginning on the occurrence of copycat violence.

We know only that the people responsible for the violent acts have said publicly to police or other authorities

that they were doing what they saw, heard, or read somewhere else. Many of them have said that the thought
wouldn't have occurred to them if they hadn't been
exposed to it through the media.

The probability of violence occurring after exposure to
violent images and themes is also dependent on the circumstances of the individual who is being exposed to the
images and themes. Many researchers believe that people
who perform copycat violence are already predisposed
toward, or open to, violence. Whether this openness to
violence comes from overexposure to media violence or
from the individual's own circumstances depends on each
individual case. Some researchers have also suggested that
these agents of violence might be using media violence as
an excuse for their actions.

Case Reports

The following reported cases of copycat violence are
examples of cases that are believed to have been inspired
by violence in the media:

May 1999, Georgia—A fifteen-year-old male was
charged with the shootings of six classmates. Prior to the
shooting, the teen had expressed worship for the boys that
killed their classmates in the Columbine High School
massacre. The teen had also said that he would be able to
shoot as many, if not more, classmates as the two boys
did at Columbine. The teen also liked Internet sites that
showed how to build bombs.

May 1998, Maryland—A twelve-year-old boy committed suicide after writing a note about the cable show

South Park. The character Kenny dies in the show, but always returns. During the same year, another boy, eleven years old, also committed suicide by hanging himself. His favorite character was Kenny, and he told friends that if he died, he would come back the following week, just like Kenny. His mother stopped the child from watching the show, but his classmates would tell him what happened in every episode. The boy drew pictures of what his friends described to stay connected to the show.

January 1998, Los Angeles—Three male youths were charged with the murder of one of their mothers. They said that the way the mother was killed came from the movie *Scream.*

December 1997, Kentucky—A high school student killed three classmates and wounded five others with a semi-automatic gun. He told police that he saw it done in the film *Basketball Diaries.*

February 1997, Connecticut—An eight-year-old died from a gunshot wound to the forehead. The gun was fired by another child. The children were "playing" by imitating a scene from the film *Set It Off* after watching it on videotape.

November 1995, New York—A group of teens robbed, set on fire, and killed a New York City subway clerk. The crime was attributed to a scene from the film *Money Train,* which had been recently released.

Your Safety

Although the people who committed these acts stated that they were inspired directly by the media, thousands of crimes and violent acts are committed without the perpetrators ever blaming violence in the media. In comparison to the many violent acts committed, copy-cat violence is rare.

Although a few of these examples occurred in school, statistics from *Crime and Violence in American Schools* by Mediascope Press show that a youth faces less than a one-in-a-million chance of being killed at school. You should not be afraid of being in your school, although, you should be aware that some teens do sneak weapons into school.

If you know of someone who has a weapon at school, do not hesitate to tell a teacher or administrator. No one has to know that you told, and telling an adult is a positive way of dealing with the possibility of violence. You might even save someone from harm by doing so.

Understanding Your Role in Media Violence

As we mature out of our childhood or teen years, the media plays an important role in shaping what we become. Adults can watch a commercial and know that their lives won't change that much if they miss the latest movie or don't buy a particular product. For teens, it's a different story.

According to the National Institute on Media and the Family, at your age, one of your main concerns is how other people—especially your peers—see you. Will everybody else get a new product and not you? Will your life be worse off without this product? Many members of the media—especially those involved in advertising— prey on these insecurities.

Based on studies and reports, FTC chairman Robert Pitofsky declared that the younger we are, the more likely we are to be influenced by advertising. Some members of the media use this fact to make profits. They know that easily influenced viewers can mean big profits. Chairman Pitofsky's study found that some media marketing plans were aimed at a consumer market as young as six years old. Think about the reality behind this: adults sitting in advertising offices being paid to figure out how to get your

Know Your Net Worth

According to the National Institute on Media and the Family, young people in the United States are responsible for $500 billion being spent on family purchases. The youth are either spending it themselves or influencing their parents to spend it on their choices. Advertisers are now aiming their projects at a new, powerful consumer— you. They also hope to get to you as early as possible.

Consider the following facts from the National Institution on Media and the Family and the Center for Media Education:

⇔ Corporations spend more than $12 billion a year on marketing to youth.

⇔ By the time you graduate from high school in the United States, you will have viewed an estimated 360,000 commercials on television alone.

⇔ Youth as young as three years old are influenced by pressure from commercials.

⇔ Youth as young as two years old are able to recognize and remember brand names and logos.

⇔ Youth age fourteen and younger spend $20 billion a year of their own money on purchases.

six-year-old brother or sister—not your father or mother, but your sibling—to spend his or her allowance on their product or project.

Various media projects aimed at your age group place heavy emphasis on having the latest clothes, looking a certain way, listening to music, having the latest video games, or seeing certain movies. According to the National Institute on Media and Family, by the teen years, friends, television, and movies become much more of a dominant source of information—and influence—in a person's life than family. This is where advertising comes in to direct your spending.

Be aware that you are a media target. Be aware that some members of the media are looking to influence you and your peers in terms of what you are, what you spend, and what you will become. Constructive members of the media understand the insecurities and problems that you face. Some members will help you to cope with these issues through helpful, informative media projects, while others will try to make profits or even fortunes off your issues and concerns. When deciding to invest in or view a media project, analyze how it's being pitched to you. A project that is constructive will not use peer pressure or gimmicky advertising tactics to get you to use or buy it. A project pitched for profit will suggest that you'll be missing out if you say no.

The Violence Will Continue

Because getting attention through violence has proven profitable to both the media and individuals, it will continue.

Many experts also believe that violence in the media is addictive. This leads to what is called stimulus addiction. Stimulus addiction is a condition where we are exposed and react to a stimulus, and develop a desire to be exposed again for the reaction it provides.

Through overexposure to the stimulus, we build up a tolerance, which is similar to desensitization. It requires more of the stimulus each time to evoke the addictive reaction. With violence, such as violence in video games, stimulus addiction requires that the video games become more and more violent to hold an addicted person's interest. Members of the media have to pump more and more violence at us to maintain our interest and to feed the stimulus addiction.

Because many of us do not know that we are part of this addictive cycle, we don't know that we should want something better for ourselves. We need to stop letting the media decide our interests and stop it from making us form addictive habits. Addictions are bad because they keep us hooked on something that we could actually live without. They keep us locked in a pattern of trying to satisfy the addiction, rather than letting us live for ourselves and our own welfare.

Making Men and Women

We look to the media for direction on a number of issues in life. The media can also, without us asking for it, direct us and our society on a number of issues. The media may be sending messages that are already part of our society, but according to the writings in *Sex Roles: A*

Journal of Research and *Women and Gender: A Feminist Psychology,* the media can also create our society, especially in relation to gender roles. A gender role is what is known to be expected of a female and what is known to be expected of a male. The media can create what our society comes to expect from men and women by repeating certain themes.

The media provides boys and men with images of and themes about how they are perceived by society when they possess or don't possess certain qualities. Some of these qualities include money, power, physical size and strength, and ingenuity. The media does the same for women and girls, placing heavy emphasis on beauty, physical size, and attractiveness to the opposite sex. According to the Center for Media Education, the effect of messages about the importance of female appearance shows up in females at an early age. The center found that 40 percent of nine- and ten-year-old girls report that they are dieting to look a certain way.

Stereotyping of gender roles in the media can be easily found in television commercials. Commercials for male youth often show boys and young male teens constructing objects, working with mechanical equipment, or being physically active. Commercials for female youth often show girls and young female teens interacting with pets, dolls, household equipment, beauty objects, or clothing.

According to a study by researchers Diane Ruble and Joel Cooper, this type of gender message—repeated over and over again—influences us to develop certain expectations of males and females. These expectations include the beliefs that males are more intellectual or mechanically inclined, and that females are meant for nurturing or for looking a certain way.

These gender messages are often combined with images and themes of violence. Examples of these combined messages can be found in advertisements in many popular youth magazines. Calvin Klein promoted a cologne for males, but released the advertisement in many teen and young women's magazines. The advertisement depicts a man with flexed muscles gripping a woman, pulling her near to his face. Her face is expressionless and vacant as he stares at her with a strong intense gaze. Another example is an advertisement for females put out by Kikit Jeans, in which armed men are restraining female models by pulling their hair.

Messages for Males

Media messages for males regarding violent behavior can be found in all forms of media. Some of these messages suggest rewards when a male behaves violently. Again, these messages prey on basic human insecurities. Try to deal with your own insecurities without falling into these media traps:

Attitude is strength—Some in the media want you to think that a strong attitude makes you a strong male. They package attitude as being a cool, rebellious, attractive quality. They want you to answer to the world and its problems with an "in-your-face" confrontational attitude. Unfortunately, such an aggressive attitude often leads to violence. You don't have to have attitude to be a strong person.

Physical strength is the ultimate—Some in the media want you to think that only the best things are associated with rough and tough qualities. Pirates, warriors, soldiers, sports figures, and other physical men are glorified as the ultimate in masculinity. Some parts of the media further emphasize male physical strength by showing physical dominance over or aggression toward females and other males. Such emphasis on physical strength can lead to violence against other males and against females. You don't have to be big, aggressive, and dominant over others to be a respected, strong person.

Aggressive heroism is desirable—The media wants you to believe that bold, aggressive, obvious acts of heroism are what everyone wants and worships about men. Some of the media will glorify images and themes of males swooping in, saving the day, and swooping back out again. Many of these characters have or are given guns and weapons to accomplish their goals. The problem is that it's still solving conflicts through forms of aggression and violence, which is wrong—even if it's for a good cause. You don't have to be aggressive and obvious to be a male . . . or a hero.

Messages for Females
Violent acts against females are far more common than depictions of females as violent characters in the media's messages. Media images and themes of violence against females have been proven to translate into real-world violence against women. Many of the instances of violence against women in the media, and in real life, combine sexual images and themes as well.

Various reports and studies, including Mediascope's *Violence, Women, and the Media* and Dr. Daniel Linz and Dr. Edward Donnerstein's *Research Can Help Us Explain Violence and Pornography,* have shown that nearly 90 percent of all rapists have regularly used media forms that show violence against females as a source of entertainment. The rapists also used media that combine pornographic images of females with violence for entertainment purposes.

Even nonviolent pornographic images of females can trigger unhealthy, aggressive sexual behavior in males. Research findings from the Attorney General's Commission on Pornography, and from researchers including Daniel Linz and Neil Malamuth, support the conclusion that a relationship exists between nonviolent pornography and antifemale behavior from male pornography users. This is when violence and sex combine in attacks against females.

This is a complicated issue, because pornographers—even the ones that show blatant violence and hatred of females—are protected under the First Amendment. Even with this protection, it's important to remember that the images and themes in pornography are not natural depictions of female sexuality or desire.

The demand for pornographic depictions of females is a result of the desire of some males to see females as sexual objects. When a female is a sexual object, she is valued or rewarded only for attributes relating to her sexual or reproductive organs. Studies including those from the Attorney General's Commission on Pornography have shown that when males see females as sexual objects, they are more likely to be desensitized toward the rights, concerns, and welfare of women. This desensitization fosters an unhealthy perception of women, and often leads to violence against them.

If it were completely up to females to depict themselves as sexual beings, most females would not choose pornography or violent pornography as a way to convey their sexuality. According to research findings, including those of the *Hite Report on Female Sexuality* and of author/lecturer Paula Kamen, women have their own individual ideas of what makes them sexy—many of which have nothing to do with pornography or a male's perception that is desensitized or unhealthy. Don't be fooled into thinking that how women are depicted in pornography is actually what is sexy about women. They are two very different things.

If you're a male, try to look beyond what the media is trying to make you value most about females. No matter what media images and themes tell you about women, no female wants to be violated or objectified. If you are female, don't compare yourself and your sexuality to those images and themes. Your rights are equal, and your body is your own. Every male and female has more to offer from the inside than the outside, no matter what the media shows us.

What You Think

In efforts to help you deal with themes and images in the media, the television industry created antiviolence programs and public service announcements (PSAs). Public service announcements are run during commercial breaks to speak to people about societal concerns. You have probably seen one of your favorite actors, athletes, or artists delivering a PSA. The hope behind the PSA is that it will reach people in need of guidance.

Public service announcements were geared for anti-violence messages after studies by the University of North Carolina showed that only around 10 percent of realistic programming showed peaceful alternatives to conflict and problems. That meant that around 90 percent of realistic programming used violence as the solution to conflict and problems. It became clear that further violence was being broadcast as the answer to the problem of violence.

Studies about PSAs showed that the ones promoting themes such as "Just walk away" or "Stop the violence" appealed to young children with little or no experience of real-world violence. Older children and teens, however, considered these sayings unrealistic alternatives to solving or facing violence.

It was also confusing to young viewers—as well it should be—when actors, athletes, and artists in the PSAs preached nonviolence, but had violence in their own private lives, or in the other projects that they chose to be a part of. It doesn't make much sense for someone to be in a violent film, and then be on your television set days later saying, "Violence isn't the answer."

Something to consider is that the stars in PSAs receive little or no money for their time and celebrity appearance, whereas the other projects are their bread and butter. Many of them feel as if the PSAs make up for the rest of what they do that might be harmful or make it seem that they believe in violence.

"I loved playing the video game called Red Rogue Warriors. *It was such a great game. It had the best*

graphics, and every time I got a personal best, it would take me at least a week to top it. My best friend Bob and I took our gaming very seriously. We even played a board game that you could buy to match the video game. We bought little figurine game pieces and painted them.

"My parents tried to stop me from spending my money on the game pieces and stuff, but I still did it. They also thought that during the summer I shouldn't spend so much time in the basement playing video games, but it was really hot outside. Sometimes my older brothers would play with us, too. We were totally like the rogues of the Renaissance. I even called my food gruel, my drink mead, and my sister a wench.

"We took the board game on camping trips since we couldn't take the video game with us. My parents thought it was strange, because we should have been out exploring nature. On one of the camping trips, they told us that we weren't allowed to take the board game with us. Bob and I immediately started brainstorming about how to keep the spirit of the game with us.

"We came up with using ourselves as the characters. We bought wooden swords and knives, and made capes and shields. We hid the stuff in our sleeping bags, and planned on 'taking back the forest from the evil Warlord.' We were so psyched about our secret plan, and my parents were so glad that we weren't mad about the game being taken away from us. Of course we weren't, we were going to become the game.

"As soon as my folks went out on the lake in the fishing boat, Bob and I suited up. We took little *leather pouches filled with snacks and set off into the woods to conquer evil. After about an hour of attacking trees and shrubs, we decided to attack each other.*

"Bob was going to try to sneak back to the cabin and steal the lantern from it, and I was going to defend it from him. A little while after Bob set out on the plan, I heard a twig snap. I inched my way towards a hiding place, making very little noise. He wasn't going to get by me, I was going to slay him.

"The sound of the twig breaking was actually my parents coming. They were surprised when they saw me in my rogue costume. My dad said, 'Oh, now this is just too much.' I hid my sword behind my back. I knew that he would be mad if he saw the sword. My parents called Bob and he came out of the woods. He too had hidden his knife. We took our costumes off, but kept the weapons hidden from my parents.

"Just after dinner, Bob and I decided to sneak off and try the game elsewhere. It was getting dark, but we could still see each other clearly enough, and the setting sun made it kind of exciting. We picked an area several feet away from the cabin so that my parents wouldn't be able to hear us. We started walking away from each other. After fifty steps we were to disappear into the tree line and try to sneak attack each other.

"After my fiftieth step I looked back and didn't see Bob. I didn't know which side of the path he had jumped to, so I remained still to see if I could hear anything. The locusts were starting up, and

were kind of noisy, so I really couldn't hear him moving about in the brush.

"Something spooked me and I remember diving toward a cluster of bushes. All I heard was Bob's attack scream as I dove into the bushes. I didn't know it, but he was already in there, in a crouched position, with his knife pointing right at me. I also didn't know that the bushes were growing out of a ditch, which was a good four feet lower than the path that I was diving from. I was now falling, falling into the bushes, and on top of Bob. I remember something sharp going into my stomach as I landed. We both rolled over and I hit my head on a rock.

"I woke up to bright lights in the county hospital. Bob and my parents were sitting next to my bed staring at me. My stomach felt sore, and the right side of my head was shaved. The doctors had to shave my head to give me stitches. My stomach had stitches, too. Luckily the wooden knife didn't do as much damage as a real one would have, but it still punctured my skin and muscles. I guess that's not too surprising; even though it's made of wood, it's still shaped like a real knife.

"The rest of the summer was spent reading books, magazines, and playing educational video games. My parents took the opportunity my injury provided to wean me off of my Red Rogue Warrior craze. For the first few weeks, I didn't want anything to do with it anyway. I felt dumb for not knowing that what we were trying to do could possibly lead to harm.

"The following fall, I did really well at school, better than I ever had before. It wasn't due to my Red Rogue

Warrior *craze. It was due to the things that I did to get over it. The books taught me things that came in handy during school lessons, and the educational games made me better at math, history, and writing. For the first time, I looked forward to being challenged by school. It's cool being a good student. I like the feeling of finally 'getting it.' I'm glad that I'm not addicted to being a rogue anymore."*

—Jon, seventeen years old.

Jon experienced an addiction to a video game. The addiction started to rule many of the other areas of his life, so much so that he didn't stop to think of the consequences of his actions. His favorite video game showed him weapons and violence, but not consequences. He hadn't thought that the knives and swords used in the game could actually cause physical damage.

You Can't Take It Back

For every action that we commit, there is a reaction to it. If you throw a book, it might hit something in its path. If you drop it and it hits your knee or foot, it will most likely hurt. The injury could lead to a bruise. The bruise might be sore for a week. These are the consequences of physical acts. There is always a set of consequences that go along with every action we choose, especially physical acts.

You cannot take away a physical act once it has been committed. Someone can say that he or she is sorry for hurting you, intentionally or accidentally, but that doesn't take away the physical consequences of the physical action. You are still in pain, and you will still suffer because of this action. You might even become enraged that the person who hurt you didn't think before acting.

Remember that feeling the next time that you think you need to solve something with violence and aggression. You can't take it back. Try another alternative—talking. You can always apologize for saying the wrong words. You can always tell the person that you are mad about what he or she did or said. Talking about things clears the air and will most likely help clear up the conflict.

If you cannot talk about a problem without getting emotional, try to take a break from the situation. Sometimes a break is as simple as counting to ten. It may seem like an unimportant amount of time, but it may make a huge difference in the outcome. Ten seconds is long enough to consider a few possible reactions and their consequences. If you cannot take a break, make the decision to have someone act as a mediator. A mediator is a person who is not on either side of the conflict, but in the middle.

The best mediators are teachers, parents, or older people who are more likely to stay neutral. Mediators work well because you will not be emotional toward the mediator as you would towards the person involved in the conflict. You will be able to express your feelings without becoming overly angry or upset.

If there are any weapons involved in your conflicts, do everything you can to get out of the situation. If you have the weapon, hand it in to a teacher, parent, or adult. If someone else has the weapon, leave the situation and tell an adult immediately. Conflicts should never be solved with the use of weapons; conflicts should be solved with wisdom, creativity, and intelligence.

The *National Television Violence Study* Findings: Media Statistics and Reality

Children's Programs—Unfortunately, many of the programs currently made for children do not show the long-term consequences of violence. Because a good percentage of children's programming is fantasy-based, the harm caused by violence is unrealistic. An example would be a cartoon character getting run over by a car, and then walking away without evidence of harm. In fact, over half of the violent actions do not involve pain as a consequence at all.

Comedy Series—Comedy programs are less likely to contain violent themes, but when they do, violence is portrayed in a humorous light.

In addition, many of the violent situations, close to 90 percent of them, take place in realistic settings and manners. The suffering and pain of the violence are seldom shown because it would distract from the humor.

Drama Series—More than three-fourths of all drama series involve violence. Only about 30 percent of those series show the long-term consequences of violence. More than a third of these series use weapons, such as guns, to depict violent themes and images.

Reality Shows—Examples of reality shows are documentaries and talk shows. More than a third of all reality shows contain some level of violence. Police shows all contain violence, whereas less than 20 percent of talk shows contain violence. Over three-fourths of the tabloid shows aired contain violence. Over half of all documentaries have some level of violence, as well. More than 70 percent of all reality-based shows fail to show the pain and harm that violence really causes.

Movies—Over half of all movies made are likely to have some level of violence. More than half of all movies that contain violence do not show long-term consequences and realistic suffering. More than a quarter of all movies with violence do, however, show blood and wounds.

Music Videos—More than half of all music videos contain violent images or themes. The violence of music videos rarely involves accurate depictions of pain, suffering, causes, or punishment. Over 80 percent of videos with violent themes or images take place in realistic settings but fail to show realistic consequences.

Seeing Through Violence in Positive Ways

The first thing to do when dealing with violent images and themes in the media is to remember that it's being shown to you for a reason. Those reasons could be to express an idea, to sell a product or image, or to further the sales or importance of the media form that is exposing you to violence in the first place.

You could also be getting exposed to violent themes and images through your own actions. Curiosity is normal, wanting to see what something is about is normal, but letting what you discover turn you into a harmful human is not normal. If a source of violent images or themes is making you think harmful, hurtful, or aggressive thoughts, talk to an adult about it.

Talking about issues is a good way to keep things in check. Sometimes merely talking about an image that you were exposed to—but can't get out of your mind—will be enough to release it from your consciousness. Talking about it will also lead to a discussion that will hopefully answer any of the questions you would naturally have when faced with a violent image or theme.

Also, if you have recently come across a violent image or theme which you were punished for or forbidden to see by your parents, please remind them of this one simple point: Banning violent material without discussing it doesn't solve the problem.

You need to be able to talk about your feelings, and to be given a chance to work through the emotions that violent material evokes in all of us. Adults need to explain to you how the images or themes are harmful to your healthy development. If a parent doesn't have answers that help you to understand your concerns, talk with a guidance counselor, spiritual leader, or teacher.

The following questions should be considered when viewing anything that contains violent themes, images, or situations. You can photocopy this list and use it to open a healthy, educational dialogue with your parent(s) or other adults about a project's violent images and themes.

⇨ Is this project reality-based or fantasy?

⇨ Who are the characters, and are they good or bad all of the time, or only some of the time?

⇨ When are the characters bad; what are they doing?

⇨ Does the project remind you of something in your own life?

⇨ Do the characters remind you of people in your own life?

⇨ What are the conflicts?

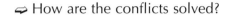

⮑ How are the conflicts solved?

⮑ Would the solution to the conflict work in real life, and why or why not?

⮑ What are other more peaceful solutions to the conflict?

⮑ Who is doing the violent actions?

⮑ How long did the character think before reacting with violence?

⮑ Who is receiving the violent actions?

⮑ How do you think they would feel or suffer in real life?

⮑ Is the victim's suffering shown?

⮑ Is the aggressor punished?

⮑ How would the aggressor be punished in real life?

Media Smarts

By asking yourself the preceding questions while being exposed to violent themes and images, you put the violence itself in the right light. You understand it for what it is, for what it isn't, and for what it should be. Another great defense against the harmful effects of media violence is allowing yourself to become a discerning viewer.

Be familiar with what you would learn from media violence if you followed unquestioningly, but seek to learn beyond what is shown to you. Look for better sources in the media that take your healthy development

Media Bias

What often occurs in the news media is bias. Bias is when something shows a strong slant toward one side of a story over another. Many producers, editors, reporters, and writers knowingly and unknowingly create bias when relaying a story to us. When bias occurs, we are not given the full story, with all of the necessary details to form a solid opinion. Instead, important information is mismanaged in order to lead us into making the opinion that is desired of us by the story's creators.

Bias occurs when a person has decided to leave out a fact or to ignore important details. You can only catch this kind of bias by comparing the same story from different news sources. Bias also occurs from the manner in which news programs and papers decide where to place stories. Stories that are judged to be more important are placed at the beginning of the broadcast, or in the front pages. You can tell which stories are thought to be more important by examining where they are placed in the newspaper or program. Examining the tone or language of the piece can also pinpoint bias. If it presents only one side of the story and uses glorifying adjectives, then you know that the story is biased. You can also read bias in headlines. Stories that are hardly worth reading might have an exciting but unconnected headline. Readers are enticed into reading the article and then discover facts were altered in order to create interest from the headline.

Bias is also found in the photographs, illustrations, and captions that accompany stories. Some pictures can make a person or situation seem opposite of what it actually is. With the right photo, a person who is generally of a pleasant character can seem to be very unpleasant. By the same measure, a person normally unpleasant can be made to seem pleasant. The photographs are used in this way to influence the desired opinion.

into consideration. Consider the following realities behind what is shown to you about solving problems with violence:

↪ *You are shown:* The problem is always someone else's, and mostly the bad guy's, fault.

The truth: The problem is everyone's responsibility and part of an ongoing situation that happens in human relationships.

↬ *You are shown:* The only solution to problems is violence and the use of weapons.

The truth: Using words—not violence—is the most effective way to settle differences and problems.

↬ *You are shown:* Violence only happens as a result of conflict, and it always works.

The truth: Violence happens as the result of the choices that the different members make instead of choosing peaceful alternatives. Violence hardly ever solves anything; it mostly leads to more violence.

↬ *You are shown:* When solving problems, there are only winners and losers.

The truth: There is usually some sort of solution that leaves everyone at least partly satisfied.

↬ *You are shown:* The same conflict will return again in the future if it is not settled with violence.

The truth: If the conflict does return again, there are yet other peaceful alternatives to try until the conflict is settled, and everyone has some degree of satisfaction.

You Can Do It!

Although parents and teachers can't always protect you from violent images and themes, you can learn to protect yourself. By becoming a discerning viewer, you can be exposed to violent images, work through the emotions that they cause, and come out the other side a healthier, wiser, and less aggressive person.

You will be able to turn off, tune out, and avoid media violence without feeling as if you are missing out. You will also learn that by watching a balance of educational television and entertainment television, you will become a well-adjusted, versatile individual for whom the world holds countless opportunities.

Choose media projects that:

- Offer a variety of issues and points of view

- Offer a variety of ways to solve real-life problems— without violence

- Spark your imagination or inspire you to do constructive, positive things

- Are educational and entertaining over the entire span of the project

- Make you feel positive about yourself and your place in the world

- Promote healthy ways of viewing people who seem different from you

Don't choose media projects that:

- Suggest violence is cool, fun, or necessary

- Encourage behaviors that are harmful toward you or others

- Urge you to imitate what you see, hear, or read to fit in

❧ Encourage violence and aggressive behavior

❧ Encourage hatred, sexism, or destructive emotions

The American Medical Association also suggests the following checklist when tying to limit the harmful influence of the media in our lives. Both you and your parents should consider this checklist. Try to practice these points in your life for at least a month before giving up on them. It takes effort and time to see an improvement, but you will notice an improvement in the quality of your life, and in yourself, nonetheless.

❧ Don't use the television set as a way to waste downtime when you could be doing something else.

❧ Discuss violent images and themes and what makes them unnecessary and inappropriate.

❧ Don't watch, read, or listen to anything violent before sleeping.

❧ Eat meals without the television on.

❧ Keep television sets out of the bedrooms.

❧ Limit the viewing of entertainment television to around one hour a day.

❧ Try to spend family time away from both the television set and the Internet.

Are You Addicted?

Keep on the lookout for addictive behaviors related to the media forms and their messages. When considering the forms of media, you can ask yourself the following questions to learn if you are addicted to them. If you answer yes to more than three or four of these questions, you may be addicted. You should seek the help of a parent, counselor, or teacher to break the addictive cycle.

- Is it difficult to go without watching television or playing video games for even one day?

- Does this form of media excite me?

- Do I get upset or anxious if I cannot use it?

- Do I use it for long periods of time?

- Do I put off doing necessary things to use this form of media?

- Do I put off hobbies, interests, and friends to do this media activity?

- Have I failed at trying to limit my own use of this media form?

- Have my parents tried to cut back my use, but I sneaked it anyway?

If you find that you are addicted, try to replace much of the addictive activities with other forms of leisure time activities. Get involved in school activities, sports, outdoor activities, arts and crafts, building models, or your own projects. Check out what's happening at the local youth center, library, and museum.

"There's not much for an urban kid like me to do . . . or so I thought for the longest time. I have traveled down a rough road, but I'm glad that at the end of it, more people didn't get hurt. Urban kids like me grow up fast on the streets. My mom left us when we were kids, so we lived with my dad. He wouldn't exactly win the award for best parent.

"My sisters and I made our own dinners each night. Dad worked two jobs, so we only really saw him on weekends. Unfortunately, he didn't have much energy for us. On weekends he wanted us out of the apartment so that he could rest. He tried to catch up on the sleep he missed during the week. He used to get really angry if we woke him up, so as soon as Friday was coming up, I'd be looking around for a place to stay over for the weekend.

"My story wasn't very different from my friends'. We all came from working-class homes, which were actually small crammed apartments. The street was a place with no barriers. We could go anywhere we wanted, do anything we wanted, without someone getting mad at us or telling us what to do.

"One of my friends, named Gayle, organized some of the kids from our school into sort of a gang. She told us all to meet at certain places on certain days. We walked the streets in a pack, feeling wild, surging energy. We challenged each other at throwing bottles at targets, climbing fences, and setting off car alarms. We didn't really start off violent, it just slowly turned that way.

"I don't really know why, but for some reason the kids in my gang didn't like it when kids from other

schools showed up on our streets. I guess it was a territory thing, although now when I look at it, I realize all of us kids had so many things in common. It didn't really matter what school you were from, you were just looking for something to do. But the kids in my gang didn't see it that way at the time.

"We listened to a lot of gangsta rap and started to dress like each other. We talked about our turf and about protecting it from kids from other schools. There really wasn't anything to protect, but it seemed to go along with our music and favorite movies.

"Pretty soon, the gang became like a family to me. If I didn't have a place to stay on the weekends, at least a few of the gang would stay out with me all night. When Saturday morning came, I'd be so tired that I'd sneak back home and crash until Saturday night, and then do the whole thing all over again. All of this I did so I wouldn't wake up my dad.

"Sometimes I was scared—not by kids from the other schools—but by the people who hung out on the street. Sometimes cars would drive by with real gang members and they would look us up and down real close. Gayle suggested that we get some guns. She said no one would mess with us if we had them, that we would earn some respect.

"Gayle, me, and her brother ripped off a television set from a parked delivery truck. We took it to her brother's friend who was in a real gang. The guy gave Gayle's brother two small guns to give to us. I hadn't really thought about it, but now I had a gun, which was a weapon . . . a weapon that could kill someone.

"About a week after getting the guns, a group of kids from another school came over to our turf. We got into a fight with them. Gayle took out her gun and started waving it around. One of the other kids took a brick and threw it at Gayle. She got mad and ran after the kid, shooting him in the back.

"The shooting wasn't like I'd seen on television or in movies. The kid fell to the ground after just one shot. He started screaming about how much it hurt. He was screaming 'Please stop,' even though Gayle was no longer doing anything. Her gun fell to the ground and she stood and stared at the bloody, pleading kid.

"One of the other kids grabbed the gun and aimed it at Gayle. He pulled the trigger and shot her in the head. Gayle dropped to ground. Three months before, my biggest worries were what to make for dinner, and now I was witnessing someone dying, and it wasn't as easy to take as they show on television.

"I couldn't believe what I was seeing. We weren't a gang, and we weren't about violence, we were kids. I didn't hate anyone enough to want them dead. I didn't hate anyone enough to see him or her shot. I didn't hate anyone, I just wanted to feel safe.

"I wasn't safe anymore, and neither was Gayle. She lay motionless on the ground in a pool of blood. I did nothing but stand and stare, waiting for someone to make it all go away. But there was no one who could do that, and I watched as Gayle died just as the para-medics arrived. The kid that Gayle shot was para-lyzed, and his doctor said that he would spend the rest of his life in a wheelchair. One tiny little gun, one *tiny little bullet, one split-second decision can change a whole human life. You don't really know how important it is to think about that reality.*

"Because of what happened in our neighborhood, the teachers and parents started making us spend our after-school and weekend time at the youth community center. They started different programs to keep us off of the street, and away from violence. I wasn't aware of it before my trouble began, but there was always the alternative of youth programs, youth shelters, and youth centers instead of violence.

"The programs taught us to stay away from hate and violence, and to not let our fears rule our actions. They taught us to learn the difference between what we see and hear in movies and music, and reality. Because of what happened to me, I get extra counseling.

"I am an angry person now. I go to counseling to help me work through my anger. I'm angry at Gayle, and the kid she shot, and the kid who shot her. I'm angry at my mom for leaving, and my dad for being so busy. I'm angry that kids like us can get guns. I'm angry at the world. But I'm smart enough to know that violence doesn't solve anything, it just takes things away from you, and gives you nothing but anger in return."

—Abella, sixteen years old.

Gayle and Abella's world didn't have to contain that violence. They brought it into their lives when they picked up the guns. A little step like that can take you from being the average teen struggling with teen pressures to being a murderer looking at the rest of your life in jail—or worse—facing the electric chair.

Violence in the real world, our individual circumstances, and the influence of media violence can converge into a dangerous combination for each of us. The choices that we make, every single one, make a big difference in the outcome of our lives.

As in Gayle and Abella's situation, and in any situation that you may find yourself in, there are other alternatives to solving conflicts than resorting to the violence that we see in the media or the violence that we see around us. There are community centers, foundations, and programs designed to help youth cope with life's issues—from dealing with media influence to real-world violence. Community programs, foundations, and centers aim to give you the coping skills necessary for dealing with the harshness of today's world. They also offer a place to go when even home isn't what it should be.

Look in the yellow pages under the social and human services section. You will find a number of services that you can use, especially under the subsections titled children's services and youth services. In these subsections you will find a number of places that specifically operate to make your life better. Many places offer an array of classes, workshops, and resources that you can use for free.

Become an activist for yourself. Make your education, state of mind, health, pleasure, and safety your most important goals. Take the time to care about yourself and the quality of your life. Try to talk with adults, teachers, and most important your parent(s) about any harmful or suspicious influences that enter your life. Be a best friend to yourself—the way that you would for someone else— by investing time and concern in your own well-being.

Glossary

advertisement An announcement that something is for sale, or wanted.

aggression A violent or hostile attack.

copycat crimes Acts of violence inspired by media violence or exposure.

desensitization To lessen feeling; to make unaware.

endorsement Aproval.

laws Strict codes that are enforced by the government and its representatives.

mass media A term used to describe all forms of media, including newspapers, books, magazines, television, films, computers, video games, and the Internet.

media violence Violence found in the forms of media, or mass media.

social codes Rules of behavior that demonstrate how we would like to be treated by others.

society A group of people who live in the same place or way.

stimulus addiction A condition where we are exposed to and react to a stimulus, and develop a desire to be exposed again for the reaction that it provokes.

submissive Weakened.

violence Force of strength, rough action, and aggression.

For More Information

Organizations

In the United States
American Psychological Association
750 First Street NE
Washington, DC 20002-4242
(202) 336-5500
Web site: http://www.apa.org

Americans for Responsible Television
P.O. Box 627
Bloomfield Hills, MO 48303
(313) 963-8000

Beyond TV
11160 Veirs Mill Road, #L15 Suite 277
Wheaton, MD 20902
(301) 588-4001

Center for Media Education (CME)
2120 L Street NW, Suite 200
Washington, DC 20037
(202) 331-7833

e-mail: cme@cme.org
Web site: http://www.cme.org

Center for Media Literacy
4727 Wilshire Boulevard, Suite 403
Los Angeles, CA 90010
(323) 913-4177
(800) 226-9494
email: cml@medialit.org
Web site: http://www.medialit.org

Coalition for Quality Children's Media
112 West San Francisco Street, Suite 305A
Santa Fe, NM 87501
(505) 989-8076
Web site: http://www.cqcm.org

Educators for Social Responsibility
23 Garden Street
Cambridge, MA 02138
(800) 370-2515
e-mail: educators@esrnational.org
Web site: http://www.esrnational.org

Future Wave
P.O. Box 6460
Santa Fe, NM 87502
(505) 982-8882
e-mail: future@futurewave.org
Web site: http://www.futurewave.org

Healing Our Nation from Violence
1300 Civic Drive, Suite 5
Walnut Creek, CA 94596
(510) 932-6943

Media Education Foundation
26 Center Street
Northampton, MA 01060
(800) 897-0089
Web site: http://www.mediaed.org

Mediascope
12711 Ventura Boulevard, Suite 440
Studio City, CA 91604
(818) 508-2080
email: facts@mediascope.org
Web site: http://www.mediascope.org

Mothers Against Violence in America (MAVIA)
105 14th Avenue, Suite 2-A
Seattle, WA 98122
(206) 323-2303
Web site: http://www.mavia.org

Mothers Offended by the Media (MOM)
P.O. Box 382
Southampton, MA 01073
(413) 536-9282

National Alliance for Nonviolent Programming
122 North Elm Street, Suite 300
Greensboro, NC 27401
(336) 370-0407
email: NA4NVP@aol.com

National Association for the Education of Young Children
1509 16th Street NW
Washington, DC 20036-1426
(800) 424-2460
Web site: http://www.naeyc.org

National Coalition on Television Violence (NCTV)
5132 Newport Avenue
Bethesda, MD 20816
(301) 986-0362
e-mail: nctvmd@aol.com
Web site: http://www.nctvv.org

National Council for Children's TV and Media
32900 Heatherbrook
Farmington Hills, MI 48331-2908
(810) 489-3177

National Institute on Media and the Family
606 24th Avenue South, Suite 606
Minneapolis, MN 55454
(612) 672-5437
(888) 672-KIDS (5437)
Web site: http://www.mediafamily.org

Parenting for Peace and Justice Network
Institute for Peace and Justice
4144 Lindell Boulevard, Suite 408
St. Louis, MO. 63108
(314) 533-4445
e-mail:ipj@ipj-ppj.org
Web site: http://www.ipj-ppj.org/ppjn-new.html

Parents Television Council (PTC)
P.O. Box 712067
Los Angeles, CA 90071-9934
(213) 621-2506
Web site: http://www.ParentsTV.org

TV-Turnoff Network (formerly TV-Free America)
1601 Connecticut Avenue NW, Suite 303

Washington, DC 20009
(202) 518-5556
e-mail: email@tvturnoff.org
Web site: http://www.tvturnoff.org

In Canada

Canadians Concerned About Violence in
    Entertainment (C-CAVE)
308 Ash Street
Whitby, ON M4W 2W8
(905) 430-5789

MediaWatch
517 Wellington Street West, Suite 204
Toronto, ON M5V 1G1
(416) 408-2065
e-mail: info@mediawatch.ca
Web site: http://www.mediawatch.ca

International

UNESCO International Clearinghouse on Children and
    Violence on the Screen
Nordicom
Göteborg University
Box 713
SE 405 30 Göteborg SWEDEN
Web site: http://www.nordicom.gu.se/unesco.html

Organizations on the Web

Accuracy in Media
http://www.aim.org

American Psychological Association—Violence
 on Television
http://www.apa.org/pubinfo/violence.html

Community Learning Network
http://www.cln.org/themes/media_violence.html

Connect for Kids
www.connectforkids.org

CyberAngels
www.cyberangels.org

Media Awareness Network
www.media-awareness.ca

For Further Reading

Bennett, Steven, and Ruth Bennett. *Kick the TV Habit! A Simple Program for Changing Your Family's Television Viewing and Video Game Habits.* New York: Penguin Publishing, 1994.

Dudley, William, ed. *Media Violence: Opposing Viewpoints.* San Diego, CA: Greenhaven Press, 1999.

Stay, Byron L., ed. *Mass Media: Opposing Viewpoints.* San Diego, CA: Greenhaven Press, 1999.

Torr, James D., ed. *Violence in the Media: Current Controversies.* San Diego, CA: Greenhaven Press Incorporated, 2001.

Winters, Paul A., ed. *The Information Revolution: Opposing Viewpoints.* San Diego, CA: Greenhaven Press Incorporated, 1998.

For Your Parents/Guardians and Mature Readers

DeGaetano, Gloria, and Kathleen Bander. *Screen Smarts: A Family Guide to Media Literacy.* Boston: Houghton Mifflin, 1996.

Huston, Aletha C. *Big World, Small Screen: The Role of Television in American Society.* Lincoln, NE: University of Nebraska Press, 1992.

Pipher, Mary. *Reviving Ophelia: Saving the Selves of Adolescent Girls.* New York: Putnam, 1994.

Schaefer, Charles E., and Theresa Foy DiGeronimo. *How to Talk to Teens About Really Important Things.* San Francisco: Jossey-Bass Publishers, 1999.

Walsh, David. *Selling Out America's Children: How America Puts Profits Before Values—and What Parents Can Do.* Minneapolis: Fairview Press, 1994.

Index

A

actors, 12, 13, 71–72
addiction to media, 40, 65–66,
    76, 87–88
advertising/commercials, 15, 16,
    24, 26, 39, 45, 48–49,
    63–65, 67, 71, 80
aggression, 3, 4, 6, 11, 12, 24,
    25, 26, 32, 35, 38, 39,
    48, 51, 53–54, 55, 69,
    70, 77, 85, 87
alcohol and drugs, 33
anger, 26, 53
attitude, 68

B

bias, 83–84
Bill of Rights, 17, 18
books, 7, 15, 23, 24, 26, 37, 48,
    49–50
break, taking a, 77

C

cascade effect, 15–16
Case, Steve, 23
censorship, 17, 27

choosing what to watch/read,
    14, 25, 31–32, 38, 39,
    40, 42, 47–48, 49, 65,
    82–85, 86
competition, 6
computers, 7, 37, 44–45, 47, 48
conflict, 6, 22, 33, 38, 55, 69,
    72, 77, 81–82, 85
consequences, real-life, 7, 11,
    14, 23, 32–34, 36, 39,
    54, 55, 76–77, 78, 79, 82
cooperation, 6

D

desensitization, 3–4, 36, 51, 53,
    66, 70, 71
documentaries, 25, 39, 79

E

educational viewing, 10, 27, 32,
    44, 45, 86
entertainment, 3, 10, 11, 13, 19,
    23, 37, 44, 59, 70, 86

F

fantasy, 45, 78, 81

fear, 25, 52
female images, 67–68, 69–71
fighting, 5, 33
film noir, 18
First Amendment, 17, 18, 47, 70
force, why people use, 26
freedom of expression, 17, 18

G
Gandhi, Mohandas, 38
gangs, 33
gender roles/messages, 67–71
guns, 53, 69, 78, 92

H
hate crimes, 46, 47
humor/comedy, 26, 31, 32, 54, 78
hype, 7, 39, 45

I
imagination, 18, 24, 38, 86
injury, 6
instinct, 19, 38
intelligence, 38, 77
Internet, 23, 37, 44, 45, 46, 47, 59, 87

L
lyrics, 41–42

M
magazines, 23, 26, 37, 48–49
male images, 67–69, 71
media, what it is, 7
mediator, 77
media violence
    effects, 33, 51–54

effects on young viewers, 24, 72, 78
questions to ask, 31–32
ways to counteract, 87
mixed messages, 31, 32, 72
movies/films, 7, 15, 16, 19, 22, 23, 26, 37, 39, 45, 59, 65
    horror, 13–14
MTV, 41
music, 7, 15, 16, 19, 23, 24, 26, 37, 40–44, 48, 59, 65
music videos, 41–42, 79

N
negotiation, 6, 55
news, 3, 7, 11, 83–84
newspapers, 7, 48–49, 83–84
nonviolent/peaceful alternatives, 4, 12, 38, 55, 72, 82, 85, 86, 93
nonviolent societies, 5–6

P
parents, 13, 22, 25, 27, 33, 55, 64, 77, 85, 88
peer pressure/desire to be accepted, 18–19, 63–65
photographs, 84
pornography, 18, 37, 46, 70–71
profit, 7, 14, 15, 63, 65
program content, 27
public service announcements, 71–72
punishment, 7, 39, 54, 82, 92–93

R
rap, 41–42
rating systems, 22, 26–28, 45, 47

realism, 53, 72, 79, 81
reality-based shows, 12, 79
Ross, Gary, 23

S
school, 6, 24, 25, 33, 40, 48,
    54, 62, 64
sex/sexual images, 22, 48,
    69–71, 87
social codes and laws, 6–7
sports, 13, 26, 40, 69, 71–72
students/studying, 24, 40
suffering, 4, 6, 11, 13, 14, 32,
    33, 36, 39, 51, 54, 76,
    78, 79, 82

T
television, 7, 10–11, 12, 13,
    15–16, 22, 23–25, 26,
    37, 39–40, 45, 48, 59,
    64, 72, 83, 87, 88

V
video games, 15–16, 19, 23, 26,
    37, 44–48, 49, 59, 65,
    66, 76, 88
violence
    copycat, 59–62, 86
    examining/discussing, 4,
    54–55, 59, 80–81, 87,
    93–94
    factors that contribute to,
    51, 60, 93
violent heroes, 52, 69

W
weapons, 26, 46, 53, 62, 69,
    76, 77, 78, 85
Web sites, harmful, 46, 47–48
workplaces, 6

About the author

Holly Cefrey is a freelance writer and researcher. She also works in the entertainment industry as a freelance casting associate.